DATE DUE

JAN 1 8 2005			
FEB 2 2 2005			

Madame Bovary,
C'est Moi!

Madame Bovary, C'est Moi!

The Great

Characters of

Literature and Where

They Came From

ANDRÉ BERNARD

W. W. NORTON & COMPANY   NEW YORK · LONDON

For information about permission to reproduce selections from this book, write to
Permissions, W. W. Norton & Company, Inc., 500 Fifth Avenue, New York, NY 10110

Manufacturing by the Maple-Vail Book Manufacturing Group
Book design by Chris Welch
Production manager: Amanda Morrison
Library of Congress Cataloging-in-Publication Data

Bernard, André, 1956–
Madame Bovary, c'est moi! : the great characters of literature and
where they came from / André Bernard. —1st ed.
p. cm.
ISBN 0-393-05181-1
1. Characters and characteristics in literature. I. Title.
PN56.4.B47 2004
809'.927—dc22
2003019445

W. W. Norton & Company, Inc., 500 Fifth Avenue, New York, N.Y. 10110
www.wwnorton.com

W. W. Norton & Company Ltd., Castle House, 75/76 Wells Street, London W1T 3QT

2 3 4 5 6 7 8 9 0

This book is for Ethel Bernard,

who taught me how to read,

and for Ramsay McGregor,

who enjoys a good lie

*Madame Bovary,
C'est Moi!*

*T*he book you are about to read is an anecdotal account of the genesis, christening, and sometimes rechristening of fictional characters of note. It is meant to be a casual stroll through the lives and imaginations of some of the world's greatest writers as they struggled to find just the right name, or just the right tone, or just the right prop, for the hero or heroine of their novels and stories.

How did Nero Wolfe end up with the name of a Roman emperor? Was Anna Karenina a real person? Why was Hercule Poirot Belgian? Why was Long John Silver missing a foot? For the answers to these questions and many more, read on. It is my hope that the little stories told here will amuse and entertain you, and will spur you on to read some of the books in question, which until now have rested quietly—or accusingly—for years on your "to read at some point" list. Some of these characters we hate; with some others we would like to have been friends, or even lovers. But above all else the characters described here are as good or even better than real. The impact they made, on our first meeting them as we read in bed or on the train or in school or on the road, has remained so strong and vivid that we sometimes feel we know them better than we know our own friends or family. As Virginia Woolf once wrote, "If the characters are real the novel will have a chance."

The great Italian semiotician and novelist Umberto Eco has noted that Anglo-Saxon literature is unique in using the names of fictional characters as book titles, and that this denotes in English and American fiction the main character's importance to the novel's progress, rather than the importance of ideas to the movement of the plot. As to non–Anglo-Saxon characters giving their names to books, think *Madame Bovary,* or *Hedda Gabler,* or *Anna Karenina,* or *Le Père Goriot.* These characters subsumed their creators, and proved so powerful in their own (fictional) right that their authors had no choice, really, but to name the relevant books for them.

So please turn the pages to find your own favorite character. I hope the account you find will reveal a new or fresh, or at the least freshly retold, aspect to round out the picture you already have of an old friend.

Adam Dalgliesh
Cover Her Face by P. D. James (1962)

*P*hyllis D. James was working as a hospital adminis-trator in London in the early 1960s. Her husband was ill and incapacitated, and it fell to James to support her family. She had had a great interest in writing, though, and so she would try to write early in the morning, before she had to begin her commute to the hospital. Detective fiction was a particular interest. "I love structure," she has said, "and the detective story is probably the most structured of popular fiction." She has also noted that it never occurred to her to try any other form of fiction. So she began a detective novel. Her detective, the Auden-quoting Adam Dalgliesh, has since become one of the mystery genre's most popular fictional sleuths. He was named, quite casually, for an English teacher James had had at the Cambridge High School for

Girls, a Miss Dalgliesh. James was later astonished to learn that Miss Dalgliesh's father was also named Adam. Many of Dalgliesh's characteristics—his penchant for literary quotations, his love of old ruins—reflect her own. And she made him a very private and seemingly detached person, one whose job allowed him to avoid becoming too involved with other people.

Alice

Alice's Adventures in Wonderland by Lewis Carroll (1865)

W. H. Auden called July 4, 1862, "as memorable a day in the history of literature as it is in American history." For that was the day the Reverend Charles L. Dodgson rowed a small boat out onto the X River in Oxford, taking with him the three daughters of Henry Liddell, dean of Christ Church: Lorine Charlotte, age thirteen, Alice Pleasance, age ten, and Edith, age eight. On that cloudless, brilliantly blue day, the thirty-year-old Dodgson, who taught

My mind was a blank except for the name [Sister Carrie]. I had no idea who or what she was to be. I have often thought there was something mystic about it, as if I were being used, like a medium.

—THEODORE DREISER

mathematics at Oxford, dipped the oars in the water, and down the river they slowly went. "Tell us a story," one of the girls asked, and he did. Beginning with a little girl named Alice, he wove a story that took her into a strange and enchanted place. Soon the day grew too hot, and the group landed to sit in the shade of a haystack. Alice asked Dodgson to write his story down so that they could all read it again. Dodgson

HOW MANY NAMES CAN ONE CHARACTER HAVE?

Deerslayer

Hawkeye

Leatherstocking

Natty Bumppo

(all the same person in novels by James Fenimore Cooper)

was happy to do so. "I had sent my heroine down a rabbit-hole, to begin with, without the least idea what was to happen afterward," he wrote a friend. Dodgson was well known for his mathematical works, some of which were extremely complex and advanced. But his fantasy life, for which he adopted the pen name Lewis Carroll, was able to unfurl thanks to the beginnings of Alice's adventures. The public was enchanted. In later years Alice, who lived a long life, who was revered for her accidental place in literary history, and who was courted by princes, grew cross about always being identified with the fictional Alice. (See under "Winnie-the-Pooh" Christopher Robin Milne's similar experience.) "I am tired of being Alice in Wonderland," she said. "Does it sound ungrateful? It *is*—only I do get tired!"

SOME WRITERS SAID TO HAVE SERVED
AS FICTIONAL CHARACTERS

John Dos Passos was Richard Gordon in
Ernest Hemingway's *To Have and Have Not*

F. Scott Fitzgerald was "poor Julian" in
Hemingway's "The Snows of Kilimanjaro"

Ford Madox Ford was Henry Braddocks in
Hemingway's *The Sun Also Rises*

Herman Melville was Hollingsworth in
Nathaniel Hawthorne's *The Blithedale Romance*

D. H. Lawrence was Mark Rampion in
Aldous Huxley's *Point Counter Point*

Robert Louis Stevenson was Ralph Touchett in
Henry James's *The Portrait of a Lady*

Truman Capote was Dill in Harper Lee's *To Kill a Mockingbird*

Harper Lee was Idebel Thompkins in
Truman Capote's *Other Voices, Other Rooms*

Anna Karenina
Anna Karenina by Leo Tolstoy (1875)

Considered one of the greatest novels ever written (and originally called *Two Couples* and then *Two Marriages*, until Tolstoy centered on his protagonist), the tale of a married Russian noblewoman who falls in love with a military

officer, Vronsky, who turns out to be a scoundrel, has been embraced by generations of readers as the ultimate account of doomed romance. Leo Tolstoy initially disliked his protagonist, whom he considered "tedious, banal," and whom he referred to as "the Devil." "She is nothing," he said. "I am fed up with my Anna, sick and tired; I am dealing with her as a pupil who has turned out to be unmanageable." But from a somewhat unappealing and difficult woman, whom he had first named Tatiana, and then Anastasia ("she is unattractive, with a narrow, low forehead, short, turned-up nose—rather large. If it were any bigger she would be deformed. . . ."), she was gradually transformed into a beautiful woman full of passion and opinion. Tolstoy noted that he wished to portray this married society woman who ruins herself not as a guilty person, but as someone deserving of pity. Tolstoy and his wife lived in the small town of Yasnaya Polyana. In January of 1872, at the railroad station closest to his house, a young woman threw herself under a train over a love affair that had soured. Tolstoy's wife related that he

*D*r. *Johnson remarked that a man would turn over half a library to make a single book: in the same way, a novelist may turn over half the people in a town to make a single figure in his novel.*

—THOMAS WOLFE

*I don't mind Marlowe being a sentimentalist because
he always has been. His toughness has always been
more or less a surface bluff.*

—RAYMOND CHANDLER

experienced "deep and terrible" feelings when he saw her body at the station, mangled, nude, with a crushed skull. Her gray eyes especially haunted him, Tolstoy's wife later said. Her name was Anna Stepanova Pirogova; she had been the mistress of a friend of the Tolstoys, and it was her gruesome death that sparked Tolstoy's imagination.

Auntie Mame
Auntie Mame by Patrick Dennis
(1956)

Most people know Mame as Patrick Dennis's vehicle for stage and screen actress Rosalind Russell's marvelous madcap performance as a sophisticated and eccentric woman of the world. But Mame began as a novel—a series of linked stories, really—based loosely on Dennis's real-life aunt. "Patrick Dennis," a pen name of Everett Tanner III, who wrote under other names as well, lived well in New York. For much of his life he had money, success, a galaxy of friends, and hosted dazzling, legendary parties, although he ended up losing everything. He had grown up in a middle-class family in Illinois, and had found his way to New York and to fame as a writer of many novels. *Mame* was his greatest success, and as soon as it became a success people wanted to know who the real Mame was. "Anyone with any sense would know who Aunt Mame really is," Dennis would say, pointing to himself. And it seems that much of Mame's glamorous life and many of her wonderful mots came from Dennis himself. He did, however, have an aunt, Marian Tanner, who lived in a brownstone in New York's Greenwich Village. The house was the scene of riotous parties, and Tanner, like Mame, went through a number of husbands. Flamboyant and sophisticated, she fit the image of Mame. But Dennis later said that the real Mame was Rosalind Russell—her interpretation of the character was better even than the original version.

Bilbo Baggins
The Hobbit by J. R. R. Tolkien (1937)

*H*obbits were born one sultry summer day when Tolkien, an academic who specialized in Middle English and the Saxon language, sat in a stuffy classroom correcting papers on English literature. Quite out of the blue, he wrote the following sentence on a blank space on one student's paper: "In a hole in the ground there lived a

Perry Mason deals with the big, masculine, provocative element of sex psychology. To bring out his talents it needs a woman who is suspected of a crime.

—ERLE STANLEY GARDNER

hobbit." Tolkien had no idea what he had written, or what the word "hobbit" might mean, and he returned to his work. Much later, however, he began to conjecture what a hobbit could be, and so began the wondrous tale of Middle Earth that has become a modern classic. (After he became famous Tolkien was asked how he had invented the world of the hobbits. "I do not remember anything about the name and inception of the hero," he said. But he added, slyly, that he would "leave the game" to future researchers.) Tolkien wrote out *The Hobbit* a chapter at a time, reading each one aloud to his sons. He struggled with names for some of his characters. A wizard was dubbed Bladorthin before the writer found a better name in the *Edda*, the ancient Scandinavian collection of myths: Gandalf, an Icelandic word for sorcerer. Tolkien named Baggins's home, Bag End, for his aunt's farm in rural Worcester. And a fierce dragon was called Pryftan until Tolkien decided upon Smaug (from a German word, *schmauchen*, meaning to fume or produce smoke) as a better moniker. When he tried to find a publisher for his tale,

Tolkien had a great stroke of luck: Stanley Unwin, the great English publisher, gave it to his son Rayner to read, and the boy reported ecstatically that "it should appeal to all children between the ages of five and nine." For the sequel to *The Hobbit,* the three-part *Lord of the Rings,* Tolkien made his hero Bilbo's nephew—but named him Bingo Bolger-Baggins. As his novels grew more and more ambitious and the world of Middle Earth deepened, Tolkien realized that a hero named Bingo detracted from the seriousness of the tale. So he rechristened him Frodo—a name out of the blue, yet hobbit-like enough to warrant keeping.

Brett Ashley
The Sun Also Rises by Ernest Hemingway (1926)

*L*ady Brett Ashley was seen by the public to symbolize the first modern woman of the so-called Lost Generation. Hemingway's account of a group of young Americans and Englishmen and women traveling aimlessly across postwar Europe caused a sensation. But he did not create his

SOME CAPTAINS

Captain Queeg
(*The Caine Mutiny*)

Captain Ahab
(*Moby-Dick*)

Captain Flint (the parrot in *Treasure Island*)

Captain Hook
(*Peter Pan*)

Captain Nemo
(*One Thousand Leagues Under the Sea*)

Captain Macheath
(*The Beggar's Opera*)

characters out of thin air. Hemingway himself had been part of the group he described, and he based Ashley on one of their number, Lady Duff Twysden. Born in England, Mary Duff Stirling Smurthwaite lived a wild life; she was married for two days to a much older man before eloping to Paris with his best man. There she was divorced, and carried on a stream of affairs while attending an endless round of parties. At the time of Hemingway's story she was thirty-three, pretty, slender, "a man's woman," according to Hemingway's wife, and very much a troublemaker. She never had an affair with Hemingway, which is thought to be a reason for his cruel portrayal of her. While the public found her fictional form fascinating, Hemingway's friends were appalled by the book, considering it a complete betrayal. The photographer Berenice Abbott claimed that Hemingway never understood women outside of a sexual context, and thus never understood Twysden, creating instead a superficial portrait. Twysden herself read the novel; her only complaint to Hemingway was that while she had slept with everyone else, she had not in fact slept with the bullfighter, as he claimed.

Is Moby-Dick the man or the whale?

—HAROLD ROSS

Carrie

Carrie by Stephen King (1974)

*A*fter graduating from college, King taught English in a high school for a few years. But he soon found that his teaching duties left him little time to write, which was an increasing passion in his life. King took a job at a laundromat in Bangor, Maine. There he found himself curious about a fellow employee, a rigid woman who quoted from the Bible endlessly. He began to wonder what she would be like as a mother, and how her children would respond to her constant scriptural allusions. The few pages of a short story he tried to write about her went nowhere—except into his wastebasket. But his wife, Tabitha, fished them out and suggested he keep trying. The short story grew longer—into a novella, which grew into a full-length novel, his first, which was taken on by a major New York publisher. The result, the tale of Carietta White and her fundamentalist mother, and what happens to Carrie after she is cruelly treated at a high school prom, launched the career of today's most successful horror writer.

*[C*haracters are] *the private museum of stuffed people that every grateful writer has somewhere on the premises.*

—VLADIMIR NABOKOV

Catherine Barkley
A Farewell to Arms by Ernest Hemingway (1929)

*W*hen he was nineteen, Hemingway volunteered for service in the First World War in the ambulance corps, which took him on as a second lieutenant. Just a few days after his arrival in Italy he was wounded by machine-gun fire. While convalescing, he fell in love with his nurse, Agnes von Kurowsky, a tall, gray-eyed twenty-six-year-old. "Everybody fell for Agnes," recalled the man in the room next to Hemingway's, "but Hemingway fell hardest." The extent of their love affair remains a mystery, although Hemingway did what he could to woo her. But in 1919 she took up with an Italian nobleman, devastating Hemingway, who was by then back home in Illinois. They were never to meet again, but this first love was turned into the doomed romance between Lieutenant Frederick Henry and his nurse Catherine Barkley in Hemingway's war novel. Many years later von Kurowsky, who eventually became a librarian in Florida, said, "It was just a flirtation."

Charlotte
Charlotte's Web by E. B. White (1952)

"*C*harlotte was a story of a friendship, life, death, salvation," wrote E. B. White. His creation, a brown spider who taught the pig Wilbur the meaning of life, has become one of the most beloved of all children's books. White found his source on the grounds of his own home in Brooklin, Maine, where he moved in 1928. He had been living in New York and working at *The New Yorker,* but he yearned for life outside the confines of a great urban environment. Brooklin,

---

SOME CHARACTERS WITH ONLY ONE NAME

Fagin (*Oliver Twist*)

Kim (*Kim*)

Charlotte
(*Charlotte's Web*)

Heathcliff
(*Wuthering Heights*)

Kurtz (*Heart of Darkness*)

Quasimodo (*The Hunchback of Notre Dame*)

Svengali (*Trilby*)

Candide (*Candide*)

Aslan (*The Narnia Books*)

Madeline (*Madeline*)

Friday (*Robinson Crusoe*)

Smike (*Nicholas Nickleby*)

halfway up the coast of Maine, provided him with the setting and surroundings he needed to write and to live a good life. There he had some animals: some sheep, some geese, and a young pig named Wilbur. As he later noted, an old rat and a spider arrived uninvited. He had been mulling over a new book about animals aimed at children. One day, while headed through the orchard to feed Wilbur, he realized that a spider he had noticed in his barn might provide him with his story. He studied her for about a year, watching her spin her web and catch flies and even bear young. And he read any book he could find about spiders, a species he had never much cared for but, after close inspection, found he liked very much. He named the live spider Charlotte, finding her to have a precise, disciplined New England-like air about her, and she soon inhabited his book. White told his publisher

There are two ways of creating a fictitious character; one, the more superficial, perhaps, is to take observed behavior and try to deduce from it the motives from which it springs. The other is to take some passing mood of one's own mind and say to oneself, if this fleeting mood were to become a dominant attitude of mind, what would my behavior be under given circumstances?

—DOROTHY SAYERS

that his spider would not appeal to those looking for a Disney version of animals. Life is stark in nature; animals eat each other, and they die, as Charlotte did. But White cared deeply for her, and for all the animals he came to see and know about his place, in the essential nature of their animal life. Anthopomorphizing Charlotte would not have produced the real creature we have come to love. (The book's illustrator, Garth Williams, originally drew Charlotte as a spider with a woman's face, a move White quickly rejected. He sent Williams to various spider guides, especially pointing out the species *Aranea cavatica* as much more suitable, and much less Disneyfied.)

the Continental Op
"Arson Plus" by Dashiell Hammett (1923)

*B*oth before and after serving briefly in World War I, Hammett worked for the Pinkerton Detective Agency in Baltimore, Maryland. There his assignments varied from looking into marital breakups to trailing men suspected of various low-level forms of crime. After serious medical problems—Hammett suffered from chronic lung illness that eventually killed him—forced him out of his job, Hammett

> **TWO CHARACTERS WITH NO NAME**
>
> the Continental Op (the Continental Op stories)
>
> the Virginian
> (*The Virginian*)

turned to writing to earn a living. Naturally, his writing centered on his experiences as a Pinkerton operative, or detective. His first sleuth was known simply as "the Continental Op," a nameless man who worked for the fictional Continental Detective Agency (named for the Continental Building in Baltimore, in which the Pinkerton offices were situated). Heavyset, plain-looking, quiet, the Continental Op never reveals anything about his personal life, or if he even has one. Hammett used his Pinkerton boss James Wright, assistant manager of Pinkerton's Baltimore office, as his model for the Op's working habits and style. Wright trained Hammett to be a detective, and advised him to stay clean, to put integrity first, and above all to avoid any kind of emotional attachment to a client. Hammett said that he didn't necessarily want the Op to be nameless, but after a few stories in which his name never came up, he found that the Op didn't need one. Because he was a familiar type of detective, "I'm not sure he's entitled to a name," he said.

No author can create a character out of nothing. He must have a model to give him a starting point; but then his imagination goes to work, he builds him up, adding a trait here, a trait there, which his model did not possess.

—SOMERSET MAUGHAM

Dantes
The Count of Monte Cristo by
Alexandre Dumas (1844)

*D*umas's account of a man wrongly imprisoned who escapes to wreak vengeance on an unjust world was based on the horrific events in a real man's life. He would have known about it from reading secret files kept by the Paris police—a particular interest of his. During the French Revolution there had been a poor shoemaker, François Picaud, who was betrothed to an orphan girl who was to inherit a small fortune. Several fortune seekers, whom he had considered his friends, denounced him as a secret agent for the royalist cause. Picaud was arrested and spent years in prison. There he befriended an Italian priest who on his deathbed told him where to find a hidden treasure, a vast fortune secreted in the cellars of a Milanese palazzo. Picaud was eventually released, at which time he recovered the treasure, traced his betrayers, and enacted his revenge. Killing two of them and ruining the daughter of a third, he tracked down the last and worst of the group, Loupiau, a café owner who had succeeded in marrying Picaud's fiancée, who had died years earlier (of grief, it is said). After surprising and confronting Loupiau, he burned down his café, killed him, and destroyed Loupiau's remaining family. Sounds like a Dumas novel? Dumas reworked the story somewhat, giving it an even more dramatic edge, but the betrayal, the imprisonment, the treasure, and the final revenge all came from life.

Dorian Gray
The Picture of Dorian Gray
by Oscar Wilde (1890)

A young man once wrote a fan letter to Oscar Wilde, gushing about his new and scandalous novella, *Dorian Gray*. Wilde wrote back instantly, principally to suggest that he and his correspondent might become friends, and asking if they could meet as soon as possible. But he included a sentence about his book that has since often been quoted: "Basil Hallward is what I think I am: Lord Henry is what the world thinks me: Dorian what I would like to be—in other times, perhaps." A cryptic comment indeed. At the time Wilde began his story, he met a clerk named John Grey. Grey was a self-taught young man, a metalworker who rose to achieve a minor position in the Foreign Office. It is thought that Wilde wanted to flatter Grey—and to aid his pursuit of the young man—by using Grey's name for his hero. And indeed Grey often signed his letters to Wilde "Dorian." When their friendship came to an end, Wilde stoutly denied ever having even thought of Grey while writing his book. The story itself, that of a man whose portrait shows the passage of time on his face while he himself never grows old, was sparked when Wilde had his own portrait painted. Upon seeing the finished painting Wilde exclaimed, "What a tragic thing it is. This portrait will never grow older, and I shall. If it was only the other way!"

Dortmunder
The Hot Rock by Donald Westlake (1970)

*S*creenwriter and comic mystery writer Westlake was stumped. He was trying to get started on a new novel, but not only did he not have a plot, he didn't even have a character to hang the story on. So one afternoon he headed to a neighborhood bar to mull the situation over. Sitting at

*Y*ou are much more likely to depict a character who is a recognizable human being, with his own individuality, if you have a living model. The imagination can create nothing out of the void.

—SOMERSET MAUGHAM

the rail, he saw a big neon sign advertising a German beer high up on the wall behind the bar: "Dortmunder Actien Bier." The name clicked instantly. His hero would be Dortmunder. He wasn't intended to be the subject of a series, but so it goes. (Westlake likes finding names in odd ways. Another series character is Parker—whom Westlake decided would never, ever be able to park a car. And he can't.)

Dracula
Dracula by Bram Stoker (1897)

Arguably the greatest horror story ever written, *Dracula* has fed the nightmares of genera- tions of children and adults, not to mention the legion of imitators that have used the image of a blood- sucking, white-faced predator in movies, short stories, comic books, and even advertisements. The model for the Transylvanian count Dracula—who is probably most often visualized by readers as the cape-wearing figure cre- ated by Hungarian movie actor Bela Lugosi (who had a pronounced accent)—is often cited as Vlad Tepes, known as the Impaler, a Romanian nobleman of the Middle Ages who was considered unusually cruel even for a bloodthirsty age. He is said to have ordered the slow death of scores of peasants by impaling them on stakes, and having his meals served at a table set outside so he could watch their agonies as he ate. One Christmas he invited many of his subjects to a festive dinner, and once they were inside the banquet hall he had the doors locked and set the hall on fire. In the local Tran-

SOME ALLITERATIVE CHARACTERS

Nicholas Nickleby (*Nicholas Nickleby*)

Plantagenet Palliser (the Palliser novels)

Daniel Deronda (*Daniel Deronda*)

Bilbo Baggins (*The Lord of the Rings*)

Peter Pan (*Peter Pan*)

Kunta Kinte (*Roots*)

Horatio Hornblower (the Hornblower novels)

Anthony Adverse (*Anthony Adverse*)

Phineas Finn (the Palliser novels)

Willy Wonka (*Charlie and the Chocolate Factory*)

Polly Peachum (*The Beggar's Opera*)

sylvanian dialect the word *dracula* means "son of the devil." Stoker, an Irishman who had worked in the British civil service, became an actor and then the manager of the great Sir Henry Irving. He tried his hand at fiction, writing several comedies and fantasies, before stumbling on the old central European legends of vampirism. He was captivated. Before long he spent much of his time in the reading room at the British Museum, learning as much as he could about Vlad and his deeds. Interestingly, the hero of the novel, Professor Van Helsing, is in his description a physical double for Stoker himself. *Dracula,* which Stoker had originally called *The Un-Dead,* was an immediate hit, and it has never been out of print since it was first published.

Eloise
Eloise by Kay Thompson (1955)

*I*n later years Kay Thompson often said that she was the last person imaginable to write a children's book. A well-known singer and song arranger who coached Lena Horne and Judy Garland, among other famous singers, she was also an actress who vamped it up in a remarkably flamboyant and colorful role as a fashion editor in the movie *Funny Face,* with Fred Astaire. Thompson was a friend of Garland's, and was asked to be godmother to Garland's

---

SOME DOCTORS

Dr. No (*Dr. No*)

Dr. Jekyll (*Dr. Jekyll and Mr. Hyde*)

Dr. Zhivago (*Dr. Zhivago*)

Dr. Dolittle (the Dr. Dolittle books)

Dr. Pangloss (*Candide*)

Dr. Petrie (the Fu Manchu novels)

Dr. Fell (the Dr. Fell novels)

Dr. Syntax (*The Travels of Dr. Syntax*)

Dr. Aziz (*A Passage to India*)

---

daughter Liza Minnelli. In the 1950s Thompson sang at New York's Plaza Hotel, where she also lived and where the young Liza would visit her. Originally Eloise was a simple game Thompson played with her friends; she assumed the role of a spoiled but lovable child who lived at the Plaza and terrorized the staff. Indeed, it is said she liked to answer her phone saying, "This is Eloise." One day her friend the artist Hilary Knight drew a little girl matching Thompson's Eloise character. Thompson, enchanted, developed a story to go with the drawing. Thus was born the little girl who has been thought of as New York's answer to Madeline.

Emma Bovary
Madame Bovary by
Gustave Flaubert (1856)

"*M*adame Bovary, c'est moi!"
Flaubert famously said—"I
am Madame Bovary." In fact,
his novel was inspired by a
real marital tragedy. In
1848 Flaubert was deeply
depressed by his inability to
make progress in his writing. He
was in the middle of a novel that
he was increasingly dissatis-
fied with. At dinner one
evening, a friend suggested that he write a novel based on a
sensational news item that was being much discussed in
France: the Delamare case. Eugène Delamare, a former medical student of Flaubert's father, was a young doctor attending the Rouen hospital. After the death of his first wife he
had married Delphine, the daughter of a Norman farmer.
Pretty and extravagant, eager to rise above her social station,
Delphine quickly tired of the provincial life of a country
doctor. She spent wildly on clothing and jewelry, far beyond
their modest means. And she had affairs with other men.
Soon, deep in debt and mired in emotional tangles, she took
poison, killing herself at the age of twenty-seven. Flaubert

seized on the idea. While on a voyage through Egypt in 1849, his traveling companion, Maxime Du Camp, claimed that Flaubert was watching the Nile cascade over a cataract when he suddenly exclaimed, "I have found it! Eureka! Eureka! I will call her Emma Bovary!" a claim few scholars believe, despite the fact that Flaubert's hotel in Cairo had been managed by a Frenchman named Monsieur Bouvaret. (Du Camp also noted that Delphine Delamare was not at all pretty, but rather plump and coarse.) But for eight years the craftsman of prose struggled with his narrative. Often working through the night, he would emerge at dawn having written less than a single page. "Oh, I'll certainly have known the tortures of art!" he exclaimed as he toiled on. Later, saying that he had had no model for Emma Bovary in

One of [the boys] came up, in a ragged apron and a paper cap, on the first Monday morning, to show me the trick of using the string and tying the knot. His name was Bob Fagin; and I took the liberty of using his last name, long afterwards, in Oliver Twist.

—CHARLES DICKENS

mind, he noted, "There is nothing in Madame Bovary that is true."

Ethan Frome
Ethan Frome by Edith Wharton (1911)

*T*he story of Ethan Frome, trapped in a loveless marriage and unable even to succeed in killing himself to set himself free, has been required reading for students almost since it was published. Wharton based her tale, which involved two lovers and a deliberate sled accident, on an accident that happened one snowy night near her home in Lenox, Massachusetts. There children and adults liked to sled from a monument in the center of town down Court House Hill, a steep incline that led into the woods. On a March evening in 1904 a group of eighteen-year-old high school students took off on a large coasting sled. It quickly gained speed, and began to veer at the foot of the hill. The driver, Hazel Crosby, lost control, and the sled crashed into a lamp-

When I'm writing, I have no idea where I'm going. People get married, and I didn't realize they were engaged. People die in these novels and I'm surprised.

—PAT CONROY

post. Crosby was killed, and her four companions were injured, one badly enough for her face to be scarred for the rest of her life. Wharton knew one of the girls—the scarred one, to whom she sent gifts and who lived on in the village, unmarried, for the rest of her life. Some years later, while living in France for a season, Wharton was freshening up her French grammar and idioms with a young professor who

---

MORE CHARACTERS WITH ONLY ONE NAME

Eloise (*Eloise*)

Alice (*Alice in Wonderland*)

Gandalf (*The Hobbit*)

Ayla (*She*)

Harvey (*Harvey*)

Ishmael (*Moby-Dick*)

Bartleby ("Bartleby the Scrivener")

Hiawatha ("Hiawatha")

Marlow (*Heart of Darkness*)

Queequeg (*Moby-Dick*)

Toad (*The Wind in the Willows*)

Werther (*The Sorrows of Young Werther*)

Chingachgook (*The Deerslayer*)

Spenser (the Spenser mysteries)

Candy (*Candy*)

Ferdinand (*Ferdinand the Bull*)

Babar (*The Story of Babar, the Little Elephant*)

Heidi (*Heidi*)

Pinkie (*Brighton Rock*)

Bambi (*Bambi*)

Jim (*Lord Jim*)

George (*Curious George*)

would come visit her several times a week. The professor asked Wharton to work up a story in French, which he could then go over to correct her grammatical errors. Wharton remembered the incident of the sledding accident, which she then wrote out in French—and promptly forgot. Years later a passing glimpse of a Berkshire scene jogged her memory. She then rewrote her story, in English this time, spending ten years fleshing it out with the characters and the love story we know as *Ethan Frome*. Wharton set the tale in the fictional town of Starkfield, but local residents of Lenox recognized the accident instantly. It is not known if the surviving friends of Crosby ever read it.

Frankenstein

Frankenstein, or, The Modern Prometheus by Mary Shelley (1817)

*D*uring a rainy June week in 1816, Mary Shelley and her husband Percy, together with Lord Byron and several other friends, were staying at Byron's house, the Villa Diodati, on the shores of Lake Geneva in Switzerland. They were a young group— Mary Shelley was only eighteen at the time; her husband was twenty-

three, and Byron only twenty-eight.
To pass the time they had been reading aloud German ghost stories to
each other. And they discussed the sci-
entific experiments of a Dr. Erasmus
Darwin, who was the talk of Europe for his
work in electricity (and the future grandfather of evolution-
ist Charles Darwin). Dr. Darwin had proposed that inani-

I think it was [John Singer] Sargent who said that,
when a portrait was submitted to the sitter's family, the
comment of the latter was always, "There is something
wrong about the mouth." It is the same with my sitters;
though they are free to talk and even to behave, in their
own way, the image of them reflected in my pages is often,
I fear, wavering, or at least blurred. "There is something
wrong about the mouth"—and the great masters of
portraiture, Balzac, Tolstoy, Thackeray, Trollope, have
neglected to tell us by what means they not only "caught
the likeness," but carried it on, in all its flesh-and-blood
actuality and changefulness, to the very last page.

—EDITH WHARTON

mate objects could be animated through galvanization. The horror stories they read led to speculation as to whether corpses could be brought back to life in this way. The group challenged each other to write their own horror stories in a competition. One night after such talk Mary Shelley could not sleep. She lay in bed, in a kind of waking trance or dream, during which she had a vision. "I saw the pale student of unhallowed arts kneeling beside the thing he had put together. I saw the hideous phantasm of a man stretched out, and then, on the working of some powerful engine, show signs of life and stir with an uneasy, half-vital motion. . . . Behold, the horrid thing stands at his bedside, opening his curtains and looking at him with yellow, watery, but speculative eyes." Starting awake, she realized that if she had been so frightened by her vision, so would her readers. The next morning she began to write what she had dreamed. It took her many months to clarify her vision of evil. The name Frankenstein (which is not uncommon in central Europe) may have come from a castle of the same name which she visited during her travels through Germany.

George Smiley
Call for the Dead by John le Carré (1961)

Short, spectacled, stout, nervous, and unhappily married, George Smiley is the opposite of James Bond. But for this reason he seems truer to life than Bond could ever be. In his vulnerabilty, his razor intelligence, and his utter normality, he is perhaps the greatest fictional creation to come out of the Cold War. Smiley first appeared in a semi-mystery novel called *Call for the Dead*, in which he played a minor character, an amateur sleuth of sorts. It took time for his creator, who had not focused on Smiley's potential, to develop him, and it was not until *Tinker, Tailor, Soldier, Spy,* a novel in which Smiley was initially not even included, that he came into his own. Le Carré, whose real name is David Cornwell (his publisher had suggested the pen name Chuck Smith, which Cornwell wisely did not choose), had been a German scholar (like Smiley) and teacher who in the 1950s became involved with Britain's Foreign Office, where he worked in intelligence, a fact he long denied. Posted to the German capital of Bonn, le Carré worked under a man who is often taken to be the model for Smiley's qualities, Sir Maurice Oldfield, the head of MI6. Other attributes may have come from le Carré's Oxford tutor, Vivian Morris, or from his friend Lord Clanmorris, who wrote under the name John Bingham. Le Carré has said that he put Smiley together "from various components—either real or imagined—of my own situation," and also that his appearance was based on that of someone who worked at the Ministry of Defence in

London, but he has never revealed a formal source, and in fact has said, "*Nothing* that I write is authentic."

Godot
Waiting for Godot by
Samuel Beckett (1952)

"*I*f Godot were God I would have called him that," commented dramatist Samuel Beckett. Since the play's original publication there has been endless speculation about the meaning of the name of the character who never once makes an appearance in Beckett's script. Irishman Beckett lived most of his life in France, and he wrote his later works in French. He once said, in jest, that the name came to him because of the French slang for "boot," *godasse,* since feet play a certain role in his drama. Another possible inspiration was the day he ran into a large group of people on a street corner watching the annual Tour de France bicycle race. Upon his asking what they were doing, he was told, "We're waiting for Godot"—Godot being the oldest (and slowest) competitor in the race. And yet another story is that Beckett was waiting for a bus at the corner of the rue Godot de Mauroy, a Parisian street famed for its prostitutes. He was approached by one of the ladies, who, when he rejected her, asked irritably whom he was saving himself for—was he "waiting for Godot," as in the street's name? The origin of Godot will never be known, and Beckett made every effort not to shine a light on the source.

Harry Bosch
The Black Echo by
Michael Connolly (1992)

*C*onnolly was studying the work of the fifteenth-century Dutch painter Hieronymus Bosch, who is best known for his masterful canvas *The Garden of Earthly Delights,* when he was a first-year student at the University of Florida. He was fascinated by Bosch's symbolism, by the demons in his paintings, and by Bosch's warnings of the wages of sin. Some fifteen years later Connolly was writing his first detective story. In putting together the elements of his main character he wanted to find a name that would work as a metaphor of a kind. Initially Connolly called his character Pierce, with no first name. But after writing a draft of the book he came across a reference to the painter Bosch and he remembered his art history class. Hieronymus Bosch became his character's "real" name—Harry, for short. Connelly felt it fit perfectly a detective who inhabits the underside of Los Angeles, a city that could represent a modern garden of earthly delights.

Hedda Gabler
Hedda Gabler by Henrik Ibsen (1890)

*T*he great Norwegian playwright, who revolutionized the art of drama, was often asked about the origins of his tragic heroine Hedda Gabler. Ibsen's portrait of a shattered marriage reverberated across Europe when it was first produced; the critics reviled it for its depressing view of male-female relationships ("a horrid miscarriage of the imagination," said one, "a monster in female form"), but the public responded with extreme emotion. Could he have known a woman in such pain? Ibsen said that he had been inspired by a German woman he had met in Munich. She had poisoned herself (not shot herself, as Gabler did) to escape an unhappy union. There were other potential sources as well. Newspapers of the day carried several stories that Ibsen surely read before writing his play. One involved the wife of a well-known Norwegian composer, Johan

Q: *How do you name your characters?*
Ernest Hemingway: The best I can.

MORE ALLITERATIVE CHARACTERS

Big Brother (*Nineteen Eighty-four*)

Paul Pennyfeather (*Decline and Fall*)

Ganesh Ghote (the Inspector Ghote mysteries)

Sam Spade (*The Maltese Falcon*)

Dick Diver (*Tender Is the Night*)

Billy Budd ("Billy Budd")

Roderick Random (*Roderick Random*)

Phileas Fogg (*Around the World in Eighty Days*)

Charlie Chan (the Charlie Chan mysteries)

Deadwood Dick (*The Life and Adventures of Nat Love, Better Known as "Deadwood Dick"*)

Marjorie Morningstar (*Marjorie Morningstar*)

Benjamin Braddock (*The Graduate*)

Svendsen, who, perhaps jealous of the attention he was getting from another woman, burned the manuscript of a new symphony he had just completed, and deliberately seduced the former alcoholic into a drunken stupor (see the play itself for the similarities). Ibsen said that he had not intended to deal with marital problems in his play. Rather, he was seeking to portray real human emotions and destinies and point out prevailing, unfair social conditions.

I made my name on Fu Manchu because I know nothing about the Chinese! I know something about Chinatown. But that is a different matter.

—SAX ROHMER

Hercule Poirot
The Mysterious Affair at Styles by Agatha Christie (1921)

A quarter-century after her death, Agatha Christie remains the world's best-selling author. Shortly after the First World War she worked in a hospital. Her husband was in the British army and was posted abroad, so to pass the time during his absence, and to earn some extra money, she took a job with the hospital's dispensary, allocating drugs and medications as needed. During stretches of free time between busy periods during the day, she found herself thinking about writing a novel. She had had no training as a writer, but she felt she could possibly come up with a good story. But what? She noticed that her job surrounded her with poisons and narcotics, so she decided to try her hand at a mystery. Her first murderer was based on a frightening-looking person she had seen on the tram on her way to work. But she needed a protagonist, a sleuth who would stand out, someone different from the Sherlock Holmes type so popular—and so familiar. Christie was inspired by a large group of Belgian refugees she had seen resettled in her own parish. A Belgian it was to be. Thinking of her own messy rooms, she made him extraordinarily neat, even fussy; small in stature; and with a vigorous brain. "I must remember that— yes, he would have little grey cells," she recalled about her invention. He needed a mighty name for a small man—Hercules, which she shortened to Hercule to be more sonorous. The origin of the name Poirot, she later said, was obscure, but may have come from her perusal of the newspapers. Rejected initially by several publishers, her first novel—and the first novel to feature Poirot—was finally taken on. Christie celebrated what seemed an extraordinarily lucky turn of events with her husband. Later, though, she thought, "There was a third party with us, though I did not know it. Hercule Poirot, my Belgian invention, was hanging round my neck, firmly attached there like the old man of the sea." He was to remain there for the rest of her life.

Hester Prynne
The Scarlet Letter by Nathaniel Hawthorne (1850)

She was the first adulteress in American fiction: Hester Prynne, the Puritan woman whose affair with the Reverend Arthur Dimmesdale in seventeenth-century Boston resulted in both a child, the girl Pearl, and Hester's being forced to wear a large scarlet letter "A," for adultery, sewn on the front of her dress. Nathaniel Hawthorne relied on some of his own family's history for the germ of his tale of sin and forgiveness. In the 1600s three of his ancestors in Salem, Massachusetts, were discovered to have committed incest: Nicholas Manning and two of his sisters. While Manning was able to escape Salem and disappeared into the American wilderness north of Maine, his sisters continued to live amidst their neighbors, both of them wearing badges that proclaimed their crime. Hawthorne often mined early New England history for many of his narratives, including legends of the Pyncheon family—the ancestors of the great contemporary writer Thomas Pynchon—for *The House of the Seven Gables*. He had been working on a version of his ancestral story for over a decade when his new publisher, James T. Fields, asked if he had anything Fields could publish. Hawthorne hesitated, given the nature of his story, but then gave him the much worked-over manuscript, noting that he hoped in his story "the Actual and the Imaginary may meet, and each imbue itself with the nature of the other." In

I don't think characters turn out the way you think they are going to turn out. They don't always go your way. At least they don't go my way.

—LILLIAN HELLMAN

the book, a very few fictional characters, such as Prynne and Dimmesdale, rub shoulders with a large cast of people drawn directly from early New England history. D. H. Lawrence remarked that the resulting book was the most perfect work of fiction to come out of the American imagination.

Holly Golightly
Breakfast at Tiffany's by
Truman Capote (1958)

*W*hen Holly Golightly's adventures first appeared in the pages of *Esquire*, to which they had migrated after *Harper's Bazaar* found Capote's story much too bold, and its language much too frank, *Esquire*'s sales soared as New York buzzed with speculation about her origins. Capote certainly based her on some women he knew in New York. Two friends, Pamela Drake and Doris Lilly, shared a brownstone walk-up on East Seventy-eighth Street— where Holly's apartment is located—and Capote liked to spend time there, drinking and gossiping. Lilly was a gossip columnist who later wrote the best-sellers *How to Marry a Millionaire* and *How to Make Love in Five Languages*. And Drake, who gave *Millionaire* its title and who loved to go out every night, later said, "There's an awful lot of me in Holly."

ONE CHARACTER
WHOSE NAME IS
ONLY INITIALS

JR (JR)

But so many women claimed to be her model that Capote gleefully called it "the Holly Golightly Sweepstakes." (Capote was sued for a fortune by a woman whose last name was Golightly; Capote dismissed her as too old and generally too ridiculous, saying that it was as though Joan Crawford were claiming to be the model for Lolita.) Gore Vidal claimed that Capote had stolen from Christopher Isherwood's Sally Bowles to produce Holly, an unlikely charge. Carol Marcus Matthau was suggested, and Oona Chaplin, and Bee Dabney, a painter, and Gloria Vanderbilt, and Honeywhile Wilder, whose obituary was headlined "Ex-Showgirl and Princess," and many others. Capote drew from his own family experience to sketch Holly. For instance, in the story, Holly had changed her name from Lulamae. Capote's

For my part, I ought to confess that I never attempted to create a type without having, not an idea, but a living person, in whom the various elements were harmonized together, to work from. I have always needed some groundwork on which I could tread firmly.

—IVAN TURGENEV

mother Nina, who had left the young Truman to be raised by relatives in Monroeville, Alabama, had changed her name from Lille Mae. He had originally called his heroine Connie Gustfman, but he found the name clumsy and changed it to the now classic Holly Golightly.

Horatio Hornblower
Beat to Quarters by C. S. Forester (1937)

$\mathcal{A}$fter a failed attempt to become a doctor, Forester spent time living alone on a small boat in rural England. He had little to do, and so he went to a local bookshop to find something to read. By chance he bought several bound volumes of a magazine called *Naval Chronicle*, a publication writ-ten for and by English naval officers during the Napoleonic Wars of 1790 to 1815. He did not have any particular interest in naval affairs (despite his tenure on a boat) and had bought them purely on a whim. But as he read into the magazines he became fascinated. The detail of shipboard life and manners, the accounts of naval engagements, and the various minutiae of seafaring men of the time struck a chord. In the writings of these offices Forester felt he had found a link with his vision of himself as a "Man Alone." He realized that he was indeed the captain of his own ship, or soul. But real life intruded. He had to earn a living. By chance he was invited to the United States to work as a writer in Hollywood. But his efforts failed there, too; he lacked the ambition or temperament to make his way in the movie business. So he sailed home the long way, via Central America. It was a leisurely voyage, taking six weeks, and during his lonely shipboard days he found himself contemplating the history of colonial Britain and its navy in the Caribbean. He recalled the excitement he had felt reading of battles at sea. He remembered his feelings of kinship with sea captains. And so he determined to write about the era, to re-create a world in fictional form that would excite the public the way he had been excited. He needed, however, a lead character, a believable figure who would exemplify the strength of Britain and the moral right of an officer at sea. By the time his ship reached England, Forester had found him, the man he called the Man Alone, a true leader. And he wanted his name to be equally memorable, something "slightly grotesque," as he recalled. "Horatio" was inspired not by the great naval hero Horatio Lord Nelson, but by the character in Shakespeare's *Hamlet*. Hornblower seemed so self-conscious, as well as grotesque, that it stuck. Hornblower was not originally conceived as a series, even when the first book became popular. However, when General Francisco Franco took over Spain

Indeed, I did name the two lead characters of [Who's Afraid of Virginia Woolf?] George and Martha because there is contained in the play—not its most important point, but certainly contained within the play—an attempt to examine the success or failure of American revolutionary principles.

—EDWARD ALBEE

with the help of Nazi troops, Forester wanted to rally the public against fascism. His descriptions of the British navy firing on Spanish vessels and repelling Napoleon's troops in Spain were meant to rally public patriotism.

Huckleberry Finn
The Adventures of Huckleberry Finn by Mark Twain (1884)

The book featuring Huckleberry Finn was initially planned to be a continuation of *The Adventures of Tom Sawyer*, and it was to take Tom through his adult life. There was a huge public demand for a sequel, so much had Tom been embraced by readers. But Twain realized he couldn't do that; as he told his editor, William Dean Howells, if he did so Tom "would be like all the one-horse men in literature and the reader would conceive a hearty contempt for

A FEW OTHER NOTABLES WHO SERVED
AS FICTIONAL CHARACTERS

Paul Gauguin was Strickland in Somerset Maugham's
The Moon and Sixpence

Gerald Murphy was Dick Diver in
F. Scott Fitzgerald's *Tender Is the Night*

Leigh Hunt was Skimpole in Charles Dickens's *Bleak House*

him." Tom just shouldn't grow up. So Twain settled on a kind of sequel, one that would focus on another young boy from the same town on the Mississippi. He called him Huckleberry Finn; Finn because the town drunk in Hannibal, Missouri, where Twain grew up, was Jimmy Finn, and besides, Twain said, "there was something about the name 'Finn' that suited, and Huckleberry Finn was all that was needed to somehow describe another kind of boy than Tom Sawyer, a boy of lowly extraction or degree." The boy was based on Tom Blankenship, a boy Twain knew well in his boyhood. Twain described him as dirty, unlettered, and starving, but with as good a heart as anyone ever had. "He was the only really independent person—boy or man—in the community, and by consequence he was tranquily and continuously happy and was envied by all the rest of us." Twain related that

Blankenship grew up to be a justice of the peace in a remote town in Montana, a good citizen much liked by the town. In later years Twain thought again of writing about his characters as adults. He had an idea that Tom and Huck should go out west and live among the Indians, and then to return, at the age of sixty or so, and talk over their lives. Fortunately, this never came to fruition. Huck Finn continues to attract attention. Even in Twain's day the book was considered scandalous, and Twain often referred to it as "that abused child of mine who has had so much unfair mud thrown at him." For its alleged racism and sexist worldview, as well as for its language (Twain would read parts aloud to his family; later his wife Olivia would rewrite sentences she found offensive for one reason or another), it is a book often banned by libraries and local school boards, resisted especially by people who have never read a page of Twain's tale.

Jack Torrance
The Shining by Stephen King
(1977)

The character of Jack Torrance is perhaps best known from Jack Nicholson's chilling, over-the-top portrayal of him in the movie version of King's novel. But there was some real background to the creation of the father who goes mad and tries to kill his family. King wanted to get out of his native Maine for a time, in order to give himself some new experiences for his writing. He and his family went to an old resort hotel in Colorado, the Stanley, a near-double of the sinister Overlook Hotel King later described. Huge, it had long hallways and was sunk in snow for much of the year. The Kings arrived at the end of the season, as the hotel was closing, and they found themselves the only guests in the entire building. At the time, King was a young father, and he often found himself getting unreasonably angry at his children for small infractions. This is a situation every parent knows—the frustration of trying to bend children to the rules of the house—and King, having been weaned on the family-friendly situation comedies of the 1950s and 1960s, was surprised and disturbed that he could respond to them with such anger. Awareness of his emotional response, coupled with the setting of the lonely old hotel, provided him with the canvas he needed.

James Bond
Casino Royale by Ian Fleming (1953)

*B*efore becoming a writer Fleming led the kind of romantic life his readers dreamed of. Born into a wealthy English family, he lost his father on the battlefields

*No character should utter much above a
dozen words at a breath.*

—ANTHONY TROLLOPE

of World War I when he was only eight. Expelled from military school, he tried his hand at journalism and then banking. His career never blossomed, but his social life did—he was known for his elegant suits, his parties, his entourage of beautiful, glamorous friends. During World War II he joined England's naval intelligence. It was there, in training and in actual warfare, that he learned many of the tactics and maneuvers that later fed his novels, including how to place a bomb on a ship underwater. His work took him to Jamaica, in the Caribbean, an island he fell in love with and returned to after the war's end, where he designed a breathtaking house he called "Goldeneye." In Jamaica he quickly became involved with a married woman, and it was while waiting for her divorce to be finalized that he began writing the first adventure to feature James Bond. His hero's name he found while leafing through a book on his coffee table: *Birds of the West Indies*, by ornithologist James Bond (it remains in print and continues to be the standard guidebook to the area). Bond seemed the perfect moniker—Fleming felt it was suitably "dull" and "anonymous," a fine contrast with the macho, virile secret agent he had in mind. For Bond's secretive superior, Admiral Sir Miles Messervy, Fleming applied the same nickname, "M," he used to call his extraordinarily domineering mother. Bond was to be "an interesting man to whom extraordinary things happen," Fleming noted. Indeed, the Bond books were immediate and extraordinary best-sellers. Fleming soon began to call his hero "that cardboard booby" but nevertheless loved him for the material success he brought his creator. Before his own death, Fleming wrote twelve adventures featuring Bond, immortalizing martinis, fast cars, and villains with names such as Hugo Drax, Dr. No, Goldfinger, Blofeld, and Le Chiffre.

Jay Gatsby
The Great Gatsby by F. Scott Fitzgerald (1925)

*F*itzgerald had already had success as the young novelist who best expressed the excitement and power of the Jazz Age when he went to Long Island to begin another novel. There, in a rented house, he could look out over the Sound and write, while spending time with his wife Zelda. The nation was in the Prohibition years, and Long Island, a colorful place at any time, was a fine home base for many bootleggers and rumrunners who wanted easy access to New York City. One such man lived nearby, and Zelda later remembered that he attracted Fitzgerald's close attention: Max Guerlach. Guerlach had a yacht and claimed to be the nephew of World War I hero General Pershing. And he had a great deal of money. A note he sent Fitzgerald asked how the family was and signed off "old sport"—which Fitzgerald used in his novel as Gatsby's signature line. Little else is known of Guerlach, but he seems to have given Fitzgerald the character he needed to make his new book work—the idea of a self-made man, a romantic who destroys himself in his quest for a meaningful future. Fitzgerald's correspondence with Maxwell Perkins, his editor at Scribner, is full of excitement about his work in progress. "I think that at last I've done something really my own," Fitzgerald exclaims. When Perkins read the novel he was captivated, and praised Fitzgerald for writing an astonishing tale. But he complained that Gatsby, as written, had little life, that he was too much of a mystery. Fitzgerald responded that he too didn't understand or even like Gatsby. But after some revisions, he was able to tell Perkins that he had come to know Gatsby better than he knew his own daughter. Strangely, Fitzgerald con-

In his creation of Jeeves [P. G. Wodehouse] has done something which may respectfully be compared to the work of the Almighty in Michelangelo's painting. He has forged a man filled with the breath of life.

—HILAIRE BELLOC

sidered Tom Buchanan, husband of Daisy, whom Gatsby loves, the more important character in the novel ("I suppose he's the best character I've ever done—I think he and the brother in 'Salt' and Hurstwood in 'Sister Carrie' are the three best characters in American fiction in the last twenty years"). Fitzgerald had wanted

> ### SOME COUNTS
>
> Count Dracula (*Dracula*)
>
> the Count of Monte Cristo (*The Count of Monte Cristo*)
>
> Count Fosco (*The Woman in White*)
>
> Count Axel (*Axel's Castle*)

to call his book *Trimalchio in West Egg* or *Under the Red White and Blur* or even *The High-Bouncing Lover,* but Perkins insisted it be named for its true hero. When the book was published and, despite great reviews, failed to sell at all, Fitzgerald blamed the failure on its title.

Jim Dixon
Lucky Jim by Kingsley Amis (1954)

*A*mis's first novel was his greatest, a comic novel of legendary proportions that continues to amuse half a century after its creation. Its hero, Jim Dixon, the hapless teacher whose utter failure to observe, let alone respect, the standard of behavior acceptable to a provincial academic community has often been assumed to be Philip Larkin, the great (and socially hostile) English poet. Amis and Larkin were close friends—they had attended St. John's College, Oxford, together in the early 1940s. In 1948 Amis went to visit Larkin at Leicester University, where Larkin was working as the university's librarian. One morning Larkin took Amis to the faculty lounge (the "common room") and left him there while he attended to some of his work. Amis was fascinated by the scene: a dingy atmosphere of desperate pretension, filled with other teachers who, for some reason or another, Larkin was afraid to offend or needed to appease. Amis remembered thinking, "Christ, somebody ought to do something with this." And so he did himself, penning a hilarious send-up of life at a small-time university. He named his protagonist for the street on which Larkin lived: Dixon Drive. Many of Amis's contemporaries swore that Larkin was an exact double for his hero Dixon, to Amis's disgust. Amis would only admit that Dixon's heavy drinking bore a similarity to his own, that "Dixon resembles Larkin in not the smallest particular," and that the unbearably pompous Professor Welch, Dixon's superior, was modeled on his own father-in-law.

By the time I'm done with [my characters], they're not like anybody else but themselves.

—JAMES JONES

Joe Leaphorn
The Blessing Way by
Tony Hillerman (1970)

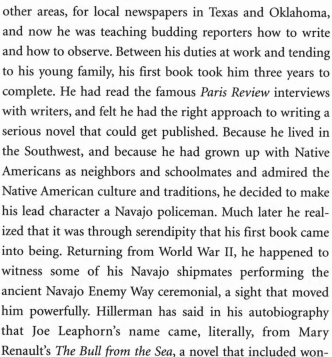

*H*illerman, who grew up in Oklahoma, was teaching journalism in New Mexico when he realized he wanted to write books. He had covered the crime beat, among other areas, for local newspapers in Texas and Oklahoma, and now he was teaching budding reporters how to write and how to observe. Between his duties at work and tending to his young family, his first book took him three years to complete. He had read the famous *Paris Review* interviews with writers, and felt he had the right approach to writing a serious novel that could get published. Because he lived in the Southwest, and because he had grown up with Native Americans as neighbors and schoolmates and admired the Native American culture and traditions, he decided to make his lead character a Navajo policeman. Much later he realized that it was through serendipity that his first book came into being. Returning from World War II, he happened to witness some of his Navajo shipmates performing the ancient Navajo Enemy Way ceremonial, a sight that moved him powerfully. Hillerman has said in his autobiography that Joe Leaphorn's name came, literally, from Mary Renault's *The Bull from the Sea*, a novel that included wonderful scenes of boys ritually leaping over the horns of bulls in ancient Crete. (The name has no Navajo connotations.) His first attempt to get the book published ended in failure when an agent suggested he "get rid of the Indian stuff." But another editor saw the potential. Because Leaphorn had become too dominant a figure on his own, Hillerman invented, for later novels, a sidekick: a younger colleague he called Jim Chee, who was a meld of several idealistic students Hillerman had known on campus.

Jude
Jude the Obscure by Thomas Hardy (1896)

*H*ardy's initial vision of his novel about a young man who could not lift himself up in life began as jottings about "a young man who could not go to Oxford—his struggles and ultimate failure." The hero was called Jack, and

Some of my characters come to me in dreams, Daddy Long Legs, for instance. Once, in a clinic, I had a dream in which I saw a man in this run-down clinic and his name in the dream was Daddy Long Legs. Many characters have come to me like that in a dream, and then I'll elaborate from there.

—WILLIAM BURROUGHS

the book *The Simpletons.* Jack was partly inspired by Hardy's uncle John Antell, a cobbler who taught himself to read and write in several languages, studied widely in science and literature, and who was clearly intellectually gifted. Antell was never able to convince a class-ridden society to give him an opportunity to better himself, and, embittered, drank himself to death. Hardy wrote the inscription for his uncle's tomb, underlining Antell's erudition and possibilities and noting that he had faced "many untoward circumstances." As the novel progressed Hardy chose a symbolic name for his hero, putting aside Jack in favor of Jude, for Judas Iscariot, deliberately invoking the image of a pariah and outcast.

Julien Sorel
The Red and the Black by Stendhal (1830)

*A*s with many novels of the time, the events of *The Red and the Black* were based on a real tragedy which was much reported in newspapers at the time. In Paris around 1825, a young seminarian was hired as a tutor for two rich families, the Michouds and the de Cordons. Antoine Berthet had no fortune, but his social and financial aspirations were great. He overreached himself, and in trying to seduce the wife of one of his employers and the young

M*any of my characters first came through*
strongly to me as voices. That's why I use
a tape recorder.

—WILLIAM BURROUGHS

daughter of the other, he found himself jobless, in disfavor, and with no prospects at all. He tried to resume his religious studies but the seduction scandal caused the church to reject him as unsuited to the priesthood. In revenge he shot the wife, and then tried to kill himself, failing in both efforts. He was tried, quickly condemned to death, and executed. The story, which was widely reported, attracted Stendhal's attention, and he used it to construct his great story of social climbing, passionless yet relentless pursuit of fame, and death. Stendhal has been called the father of the naturalistic school for his coolly detached, straightforward narratives, which were in extreme contrast to the kind of fiction then being written. Sorel's life is a near-double for that of Antoine Berthet, as is his eventual fate. But contemporary readers realized that many of Sorel's characteristics—his brilliant conversation, his courage, his phenomenal memory, his ambition—and his physical characteristics—his dark hair, his slender build, his black eyes—were exactly modeled on Stendhal himself.

Kinsey Milhone
A Is for Alibi by Sue Grafton (1982)

*F*rom an early age Sue Grafton loved the hard-boiled writers such as Dashiell Hammett and Ross Macdonald. She wanted to follow in their footsteps, but with a female protagonist. "I'm female and I figured it was my one area of expertise," she has said. A former medical secretary who wrote at night after her children were asleep, she began the Milhone series without knowing much about the actual life of a private investigator, so she studied forensics, toxicology, arson, anatomy, and everything else she could find that would add to her knowledge of the investigator's world. The name Kinsey she spotted in a newspaper column reporting births; a couple had named their baby Kinsey and Grafton was so taken with it she clipped the article for future use. Milhone was found either in the telephone book or in someone's obituary. Grafton has often said that Milhone is her

A writer can give an illusion of depth by giving an apparently stereoscopic view of a character—seeing him from two vantage points; all a writer can do is give more or less information about a character, not information of a different order.

—EVELYN WAUGH

alter ego. The two share many characteristics and even many material objects. Milhone's guns, her pale blue dented Volkswagen, the all-purpose dress—all are Grafton's. Grafton has worked to make Milhone capable, plainspoken, independent, and textured. "I like her inconsistencies and flaws just as much as I admire her fine qualities," says Grafton. "Where does this stuff come from? Wish I knew. I'd bottle it instead of reinventing myself every time."

Kurtz
Heart of Darkness by Joseph Conrad (1902)

"Mistah Kurtz, he dead," wrote Conrad in the most famous line from his astoundingly powerful book about oppression, imperialist dread, and alienation from civilization. But who was Kurtz? He remained an enigma even to his subjects in the book. In 1890 Conrad, a Polish sailor who learned English relatively late in his life—and who became one of the greatest masters of English prose—was hired to command a boat headed into the Belgian Congo on a hunt for valuable minerals. The journey was long and extremely depressing. Conditions in colonial Africa were worse than anyone from the outside world had even imagined; there was a proliferation of disease, the Belgian colonial administrators were savage and sadistic, and the native population was brutally oppressed. Conrad kept a

> **TWO SETS OF BROTHERS**
>
> Sherlock and Mycroft Holmes
> (the Sherlock Holmes stories)
>
> Dmitri, Ivan, and Alexei Karamazov
> (*The Brothers Karamazov*)

diary of his trip, and as he progressed deeper into the heart of the continent, and deeper into the clouds of fog that shrouded the great rivers, he grew more afraid and more gloomy about the future of man. "No sleep," in a frequent entry. "Fell considerably in doubt. . . ." Upon his return to Europe he began to try to describe the full horrors of what he had seen in fictional form. As often with Conrad, the tale was narrated by Marlow, Conrad's alter ego. But the main character was Kurtz, the insane European ("all Europe contributed to the making of Kurtz") who lived the life of a savage king in the jungle. Kurtz was originally called Klein, but eventually Conrad switched to a more anonymous and vague middle-European name, Kurtz. (Interestingly, while *klein* means "small" in German, "*kurz*" or its old-fashioned variant, "*kurtz*," means "short.") Several colonial settlers, whom Conrad would have seen or heard about on his hellish trip, have been put forth as models. There was a German doctor, Eduard Schnitzer, a Jew who converted to Protestantism and then, in Africa, converted again to Islam and changed his name to Emir Pasha. Pasha wielded considerable genuine political power as a governor of a Sudanese province; he then formed his own private kingdom, in which he dealt in vast quantities of ivory. Eventually he was brought back to Europe, and to the "civilized" world, by the explorer Henry Stanley. There was a Belgian official named Hodister, another ivory dealer who was eventually murdered by a local tribe leader and who had his head publicly displayed on a post (as Kurtz does with his enemies in the book). There was Guillaume van Kerckhoven, a Belgian police officer who was also fond of putting his enemies' heads on stakes, as did the much feared Georges Antoine Klein, a Belgian station chief at Stanley Falls. Unfortunately, Conrad had no lack of murderous officials run amok from whom he could borrow traits and events.

The Little Prince
The Little Prince by Antoine de Saint-Exupéry (1943)

*F*rench aviator Saint-Exupéry was living in New York City during the initial years of World War II, and he stayed on in self-imposed exile after France fell to the Nazis. He had already embarked on a successful writing career, having won the National Book Award for his adventure narrative *Wind, Sand and Stars*. For a decade he had been illustrating letters, margins of other books, and even table-cloths with a cartoon figure he called "the little lonely man," a short, strange figure with thinning hair. His American publisher suggested he write a children's book centering on this image. Saint-Exupéry fell in love with the concept, and immediately went to a drugstore where he bought a children's watercolor paint set. The story flowed from his pen with ease; it was the illustrations that proved difficult. The little man took one form, and then another. Inspiration came when he spied a doll at the apartment of a close friend. Modeling his figure on the doll, he added a full head of curly hair and a cherubic mien. (The same friend's poodle served as the model for the sheep in the eventual book.) Using the serial number of his airplane in his nonfiction account *Southern Mail* (B-612) for the name of the little man's asteroid, and basing the Rose on his wife Consuelo, Saint-Exupéry brought *The Little Prince* to life. The author later said that he had looked down at a blank sheet of paper and saw his prince hovering. "I asked him who he was," said the author. "I'm the Little Prince" was the reply. Saint-Exupéry disappeared over the Mediterranean while on a flight to Africa in 1943; his fate is still a mystery. He thus never embarked on the project he wished to pursue next: *The Little Princess*.

Character is arguably the most important single component of the novel. . . . Nothing can equal the great tradition of the European novel in the richness, variety and psychological depth of its portrayal of human nature.

—DAVID LODGE

Lolita
Lolita by Vladimir Nabokov (1955)

*V*ladimir Nabokov, who was born into an aristocratic, politically active Russian family, fled his homeland during the Russian Revolution of 1917. After some time spent in England and in Berlin, in the late 1930s the nomadic exile found himself in Paris. One day he read an article in a newspaper telling of a monkey who, from his cage in the Paris zoo, had made the first drawings known to have been created by an animal. (The images were of the bars on the monkey's cage.) Nabokov later said there was "no textual connection" between the piece he read and his train of creative thought, but he began to sketch out a story about a man who marries the mother of a young girl, and who after his wife's death tries to seduce the girl. The man, who in the germ of Nabokov's story then kills himself, was named Arthur. Nabokov destroyed his story, but some years later returned to the same theme, and worked up a novel in which

the young girl was named Juanita Dark. By 1954 he had finished his novel—then called *The Kingdom by the Sea*—and
tried to find a publisher. His novel was rejected everywhere;
publishers who were scandalized by the overt implications of
what they read as pornography and child seduction. "Lolita
has no moral in tow," the author said, and he often claimed
the true intent of his book was to testify to his love affair not
with young girls but with the English language. But in the
1950s such a book could not be published easily. He found a
publisher in Paris, the Olympia Press, which specialized in
taking on what others would not. His novel, *Lolita*, was the
book that made him famous and rich, and which introduced
a new term in English for a seductive young girl.

*The legend that characters run away from their
authors—taking up drugs, having sex operations, and
becoming president—implies that the writer is a fool with
no knowledge of his craft. This is absurd. . . . The idea of
authors running around helplessly behind their
cretinous inventions is contemptible.*

—JOHN CHEEVER

Long John Silver
Treasure Island by Robert Louis Stevenson (1881)

*O*ne rainy September morning in 1886, to pass the time, Robert Louis Stevenson opened his young son Lloyd's watercolor box and, together with the boy, began to draw an imaginary island. They filled in the bays and mountains, and as they drew, Stevenson made up the beginnings of a story about the island to his boy. Lloyd wanted to use the map as a plaything, but Stevenson felt strangely drawn to his creation. Taking it up to his bedroom, he examined it closely. As he did so, he later recalled, "the future characters of the book began to appear there visibly among imaginary woods, and their brown faces and bright weapons peeped out at me from unexpected quarters, as they passed to and fro, fighting and hunting treasure." He wrote one chapter of his new story at a time, reading it aloud to his son and his father. Within two weeks it was completed, and Stevenson was convinced he had written, as he had set out to do, "the *best* book about the Buccaneers that can be had." It was originally called *The Sea-Cook*, for the main character was to be not young Jim Hawkins, the lad who falls prey to the pirates' greed for gold, but the ship's cook, a one-legged, ferocious, powerfully built, and cunning devil: Long John Silver, the crippled leader of the story's mutinous brigands (who called him "Barbeque"). Long John was closely modeled on Stevenson's school chum William Ernest Henley, a pugnacious, gregarious fellow who had had a foot amputated as a boy. Henley spent much of his time at school in bed, as an invalid recovering from various illnesses. Stevenson wrote him, when presenting him with a finished copy of the tale, "It was the sight of your maimed strength and masterfulness that begat Long John in *Treasure Island*. . . . [T]he idea of the maimed man, ruling and dreaded by sound, was entirely taken from you." (He also noted, "If this don't fetch the kids, why, they have gone rotten since my day.") Henley loved Long John, as did Stevenson, who later wrote, "To this day I rather admire that smooth and formidable adventurer."

Lord Jim
Lord Jim by Joseph Conrad (1900)

*T*he master of evoking the imperialist nightmare used his omniscient narrator, Marlow, once again to tell a story of cowardice and redemption that Conrad took, in broad terms, from a real incident. In August 1890 a badly crowded steamship, the *Jeddah*, left Singapore headed for Arabia carrying 953 Muslim pilgrims. Not far from its destination the ship had an accident of a kind; the boat began to leak and appeared to founder. Its officers, including its captain, decided to abandon the ship—which they did, without first ensuring the safety or well-being of any of its passengers. They managed to reach the port city of Aden, where

Unless you are deliberately creating a superior type,
which distinctly appeals to the juvenile mind, the reader
loses sympathy with a character who becomes too
invincible. A reader likes to identify himself with
the central character.

—ERLE STANLEY GARDNER

they reported the ship had sunk and all on board drowned. The very next day, the *Jeddah* itself appeared at Aden; the ship had not sunk, but had been rescued, together with all the passengers, and had been towed to port by its rescuing vessel. The scandal was worldwide and instantaneous. Not the least part of it was the shame of a captain and his crew abandoning a vessel and nearly one thousand human beings to their fate on the open sea. Their penalty was light, however; after a trial Captain Clark's skippering license was suspended for a few years. His first mate, Augustine Williams, was only reprimanded. Conrad, who met Williams by chance in Singapore while traveling some years after the tragedy, drew on Williams as his exact model for Jim, who must live with his cowardice for the rest of his life. As he noted in a letter, "A charge of neglect and indifference in the matter of saving lives is the cruelest blow that can be aimed at the character of a seaman." Conrad invested Jim with

Williams's family background as well as his eventual life in the Far East, married to a Eurasian and living a life of penance.

Madeline
Madeline by Ludwig Bemelmans (1949)

*A*ustrian-born Bemelmans was many things in his life: waiter, artist, gourmet, elegant describer of society life for *The New Yorker*, man-about-town, humorist, style icon. But he is best loved and remembered for his series of children's books centered on the irrepressible Madeline, the fearless adventurer who says "pooh, pooh" to tigers in the zoo. Madeline was "born" during a vacation Bemelmans took with his wife and daughter on the tiny island of Yeu, off the west coast of France. In the idyllic setting of the little fishing harbor thronged with sardine boats and tuna schooners, Bemelmans was hit by the island's only car as he rode his bicycle. His hospital room had a crack in the ceiling that looked like a rabbit, and the patient in the next room

> **THREE CHARACTERS WITH METALLIC ELEMENTS IN THEIR NAMES**
>
> Long John Silver (*Treasure Island*)
>
> David Copperfield (*David Copperfield*)
>
> Auric Goldfinger (*Goldfinger*)

was a little girl waiting to have her appendix removed. "I saw the nun bringing soup to the little girl. I remembered the stories my mother had told me of life in the convent school at Altotting and the little girl, the hospital, the room, the crank on the bed, the nurse, the old doctor, all fell into place." Upon his recovery and return to New York, where he lived, he wrote out the story's first lines on the back of a menu at Pete's Tavern, one of the city's oldest bars and famous for serving as journalist and short story master O. Henry's home away from home.

Maigret
The Case of Peter the Lett by Georges Simenon (1931)

*I*n 1930 Georges Simenon was living on a boat, the *Ostrogoth*, anchored off the coast of Holland. Twenty-seven years old, he had already published several hundred pulp novels. Simenon later remembered that, while trying to write a new novel and nursing a drink, a bulky figure gradually seemed to appear to him as he sat on his boat. This figure, it was clear, could be a fine fictional character. In developing him Simenon had no plans to make him a series character, but Maigret's popularity was such that Simenon ended up writing 102 Maigret novels at a pace of four to six a year. Simenon had known several people named Maigret, including a police officer he had had dealings with in Belgium while working as a journalist. Many of Maigret's qualities were based on Simenon's own habits—his pipe smoking, his love of good food and drink, his pensiveness. The author admitted that Maigret was a character who was not concocted out of thin air but resembled his creator. Later Simenon worried, only half joking, that the ever-patient Maigret had grown too big for his creator, and that "he is about to become more important than I am."

Mary Poppins
Mary Poppins by P. L. Travers (1934)

"I think the idea of Mary Poppins has been blowing in and out of me, like a curtain at a window, all my life," Travers told an interviewer. An Australian of Irish descent, she was born Helen Lyndon Goff, but, intensely pri-

I was writing a story about two young men, Bertie Wooster and his friend Corky, getting into a lot of trouble. I thought: well, how can I get them out? And I thought: suppose one of them had an omniscient valet? I wrote a short story about [Jeeves], then another short story, then several more short stories and novels. That's how a character grows.

—P. G. WODEHOUSE

vate, she later adopted the pseudonym Pamela Lyndon Travers when she began a life as a stage actress. As a young woman she fell in love with Celtic traditions and with Eastern mysticism, which fueled her interest in magic and the interplay of man and nature. One day, while living in an ancient thatched cottage in Sussex, England, she found herself trying to entertain two bored young visitors. Casting about for a story to tell them, she imagined a pink-cheeked governess who comes to 17 Cherry Lane in London to care for the Banks family. As a published book, *Mary Poppins* was a spectacular success, inspiring numerous sequels as well as the Disney movie. "I have always assumed, when I thought about it at all, that she had come out of the same wall of nothingness as the poetry, myth and legend that had absorbed me all my writing life," Travers wrote.

Miss Havisham
Great Expectations by Charles Dickens (1860–61)

While, as with almost all of Dickens's unmatchable characters, there was no exact model for the bitter Miss Havisham, he certainly knew a number of women whose fates, and whose clothing—all white—paralleled hers. As a child he knew of "the White Woman" of Berners Street in London, a madwoman who dressed all in white, her head shrouded in a white bonnet and veil. And he remembered

A *real character in one of my books*
sticks out like a sore thumb.

—P. G. WODEHOUSE

Martha Joachim, who dressed herself in white after her fiancé shot himself in her presence. His close friend Wilkie Collins had lived for years with Caroline Graves until she left him for another man; Graves liked to dress in white, and was thought to have inspired Collins's huge best-seller *The Woman in White*. Collins's success with *White* prompted Dickens to compete with his own *Great Expectations*. And he read in the newspapers of the murder of a French duchess who lived in seclusion in a vast darkened mansion on the Champs-Elysées. These various elements gave him the physical outline of the woman who had been jilted at the altar and lived her life consumed by revenge and self-hatred.

Miss Lonelyhearts
Miss Lonelyhearts by Nathanael West (1933)

While trying to break out as a writer, West worked as a night clerk at the Kenmore Hall Hotel in New York City. One evening his friend S. J. Perelman, a writer for *The New Yorker* who was dating West's sister, stopped by and suggested West come out for dinner. Perelman was bringing along someone he knew, a woman who wrote an advice column for a Brooklyn newspaper. The woman, whose column was called "Susan Chester" (much like that of the late Ann Landers), showed West and Perelman some letters she found herself unable to answer—the small tragedies her correspondents cited were too much for her. Perelman found them "too depressing to be parodied in my inimitable style," but West was fascinated, and knew he had found inspiration for a new book. The name of his main character, who was to be a man who answered letters for an advice column, came to him immediately—it seemed a name absurd and tragic enough to fit an advice column for the lovelorn. He read aloud as he wrote, trying to find the perfect emotional pitch. And he found that the down-at-the-heels residents and guests staying at the Kenmore Hall Hotel were almost too similar to the people he was trying to write about —they were suffocating, even as they inspired. The eventual book, like its characters, was a failure commercially, though it has gradually come to be seen as an American masterpiece.

Miss Marple
Murder at the Vicarage by Agatha Christie (1930)

Agatha Christie had already become famous for her series of mysteries featuring the Belgian detective Hercule Poirot when Miss Marple appeared in her imagination. She had earlier written *The Murder of Roger Ackroyd,* in which an unmarried elderly woman named Caroline had a somewhat minor role in the story. But Christie remembered her as her own favorite character in that book. Reluctant to lose her, Christie used this woman in slightly different form for a series of short stories she wrote. They were set in rural English villages and featured the kind of people Christie had grown up with: genteel, comfortable older women surrounded by chintz. The main character in the first tale was renamed Miss Jane Marple, whom Christie described as "fussy and spinsterish." Much of Miss Marple's character was based on Christie's own grandmother. She was cheerful, but always suspected the worst of people and events. And she was almost always right. "Miss Marple insinuated herself so quietly into my life that I hardly recognized her arrival," Christie later wrote. "Certainly at the time I had no intention of continuing her for the rest of my life. I did not know that she was to become a rival to Hercule Poirot." Miss Marple shared one important characteristic with Poirot—at her creation she was already old. Christie often

*Distrusting writers as heroes,
I made Bech as unlike myself as I could.*

—JOHN UPDIKE

worried how to treat the passage of time with both of her inventions as they went on to new adventures in successive novels—a situation she solved by not alluding to the waning years in any way.

Mr. Hyde

Strange Case of Dr. Jekyll and Mr. Hyde by Robert Louis Stevenson (1886)

Stevenson was sleeping badly one week, tossing and unable to find rest. One night, having finally fallen asleep, he cried out violently. His wife Fanny immediately woke him—to Stevenson's dismay. "I was dreaming of a fine bogey tale," he complained. He had, in his sleep, conceived of a terrible story of human transformation. His characters were clear, and he had dreamed of their progress up to the hideous scene of Dr. Jekyll's transformation into the monstrous Mr. Hyde when he was awakened. The following morning he began writing out his tale, which he finished within three days. But Fanny, greatly distressed by the shocking story she read, remonstrated with him that, instead of a masterpiece, he had written sensationalist pulp which would ruin his reputation as a writer. Stevenson instantly flung his manuscript into the fire and began again, locking himself in his room. Beset by fever, he wrote furiously and fast. A somewhat toned-down version emerged just a few days later, and that is the version we recognize as the classic horror story. The chronically ill Stevenson, who called his Hyde "a Gothic gnome" who "came out of a deep mine," had been under the influence of drugs when he dreamed, and then wrote, his story. A form of opium had been prescribed for his respiratory illnesses. Some biographers suggest that Stevenson's constant exposure to toxins, which certainly transformed his own behavior, clouded his mind and provoked his imagination toward dark visions of double identity and man's constant struggle with good against evil.

Moby-Dick
Moby-Dick by Herman Melville (1851)

*I*t is the great American novel, the book that covers all themes, the volume that changed American fiction forever. The novel sprang from Melville's genius, but it had its source in a real white whale, a ferocious beast known to attack vessels in the Pacific Ocean. Mocha Dick was its nickname; all whalers knew of it, and many feared its power. Melville learned of Mocha Dick from a famous account of an encounter with this whale, or one

War and Peace *had, in my judgment, almost not*
reached perfection because of the difficulty I had
experienced in identifying the characters by their name.

—C. S. FORESTER

very like it: the narrative of Owen Chase. Chase had been a
crewman on the whaleship *Essex*, which in 1820 was hunting
whales off the coast of Ecuador. The crew harpooned a huge
whale which, to their horror, turned on the ship in a rage and
attacked it. Rammed twice, the *Essex* quickly sank, leaving
Chase and his mates to drift on the open ocean hundreds of
miles from shore. Only five men survived to tell their tale,
which included gruesome accounts of exposure and canni-
balism. Chase's published tale of the disaster found a wide
audience. Years later Melville was told the story by a young
sailor who turned out to be Chase's son. Fascinated, Melville
read the log Chase had written. "The reading of this wondrous story upon the landless sea, & close to the very latitude
of the shipwreck, had a surprising effect on me," he wrote.
Simultaneously he was reading Thomas Carlyle's account of
the rigid, tyrannical English Lord Protector Oliver
Cromwell, who gave him a model for the obsessed Captain
Ahab. For several years Melville worked on his own fictional
version of Chase's tale, struggling with the right tone. "Blub-

ber is blubber you know," he wrote to a friend. "Tho' you may get oil out of it, the poetry runs as hard as sap from a frozen maple tree—and to cook the thing up, one must needs throw in a little fancy. . . . I mean to get to the truth of the thing, spite of this." But on he worked to produce the great novel. When it was published, it was demolished by the critics, and found no readers at all. The British edition was issued not for adults but as a children's book—and that failed miserably as well. A century later William Faulkner said that the only book he thought was perfect as written was *Moby-Dick*.

Nero Wolfe
Fer-de-Lance by Rex Stout (1933)

*T*he prolific Rex Stout always started a new book by drawing up a list of characters and their potential names. In 1933 he had already published several books. A week after his daughter was born, he decided to start with a new mystery and a new hero. Wolfe seemed to appear out of thin air. "He was born," Stout later said, "and he was inspired neither from a chapel

*M*ost of my novels show what happens around one
character. The other characters are always seen by him.
So it is in this character's skin I have to be. And it's
almost unbearable after five or six days. That is one of
the reasons my novels are so short.

—GEORGES SIMENON

nor a bordello." Stout didn't need to think up his eye color or
his height or his profile. "He does what he pleases." But he
did need a memorable name for his fat, flower-loving, gour-
mand character. And he seems to have drawn on his own
name for inspiration. *Rex* means king in Latin—so Stout
chose the name of a Roman emperor, Nero. Stout knew
nothing of law or crime when he began to write about Nero
Wolfe, nor did he pursue any research. He liked to tell aspir-
ing writers that the best method for successful writing was,
"Apply the seat of the pants to the seat of the chair, and go."
To add to his books' appeal, Stout added a sidekick for Wolfe,
Archie Goodwin. Initially his publisher found Archie to be
too much of a Dr. Watson figure. But Stout loved them both.
Friends of Stout's saw strong elements of the author in both
characters. For instance, Wolfe and Stout shared many of the
same likes (Jane Austen, milk, crossword puzzles) and dislikes (Webster's Third New International Dictionary, ice

water, paper plates). Wolfe was such an outsized, somewhat outrageous figure that a prominent critic of the time, Alexander Woollcott (who inspired the unlovable guest in *The Man Who Came to Dinner*) swore that he himself was the model. Stout denied it, but Woollcott took to addressing his own secretary as "Archie."

Nora Charles
The Thin Man by Dashiell Hammett
(1932)

*D*ashiell Hammett once said that all of his characters were real, and were all based directly on people he knew. To his friends who read his last novel, *The Thin Man*, protagonists Nora Charles and her husband Nick were instantly recognizable as Hammett himself and his longtime companion, playwright Lillian Hellman. Both were regulars on the cocktail circuit in New York, both were exactly the ages of Nick and Nora, and their relationship was clearly the model for Nora and Nick's banter. Hellman was delighted to be seen as the real-life Nora, but Hammett told her not to be so cocky. According to him, not only was she Nora, she was also the model for the villainess (whose identity will not be revealed here). Later Hellman said that she saw little of herself in Nora, but that Nora represented Hammett's idealized version of her.

Perry Mason
The Case of the Velvet Claws
by Erle Stanley Gardner (1933)

*G*ardner had made a successful career writing stories for pulp publications, many of them, because he was so prolific, under pseudonyms. But he wanted to write a full-length mystery novel and he knew from the beginning he wanted to feature a lawyer as his hero. He had had enough of the hard-boiled detectives familiar to the reading public. To make his name, he needed a new, previously unexploited approach to a traditional genre. His first try was named Ed Stark, a lawyer who had a secretary named Della Street. Stark was an enigmatic man, quiet, something of a brown study. Della was already fully sketched: efficient, a bit thrown by her boss, with a "hint of weariness at the corner of her eyes." Stark seemed wooden, though. Gardner's editor complained that he lacked vitality. Gardner shook him up a bit, adding nuances to Stark's character, rounding him out more, and calling him Ed Stone, to give the impression of strength and durability. Then Gardner morphed Stone into Mason—a natural train of thought, as a mason works with stone and shapes his surroundings with care and skill. He wanted his hero to be a fighter who didn't shrink from a battle, a man of infinite patience who would always secure victory. And, he said, "I want to have characters who start from scratch and sprint the whole darned way." Bedeviled all his life by com-

*My favorite characters are Sarah Gamp—a cruel,
ruthless woman, a drunkard, opportunist, unreliable,
most of her character was bad, but at least it was
character; Mrs. Harris, Falstaff, Prince Hal, Don Quixote,
and Sancho, of course. Lady Macbeth I always admire.
And Bottom, Ophelia, and Mercutio—both he and
Mrs. Gamp coped with life, didn't ask any favors, never
whined. Huck Finn, of course, and Jim. Tom Sawyer
I never liked much—an awful prig.*

—WILLIAM FAULKNER

parisons to Dashiell Hammett, whose hard-boiled approach
Gardner wanted to avoid, Gardner virtually invented the
courtroom drama; his novels about Perry Mason secured the
lawyer as hero in the image of the public, who did, after all,
want what Gardner had predicted: dependability, a straightforward narrative, and a no-nonsense, frill-free protagonist.
Raymond Chandler later wrote of Gardner's creation, "Perry
Mason is the perfect detective because he has the intellectual
approach of the juridical mind and at the same time the
restless quality of the adventurer who won't stay put. I think
he is just about perfect."

Peter Pan
Peter Pan by J. M. Barrie (1904)

*A*s a young married playwright J. M. Barrie liked to walk his Newfoundland dog in London's Kensington Gardens. Often he would see a small group walking the same route: a nanny with three young children in her charge. The dog quickly attracted the children's attention, as dogs do, and before long acquaintance grew into friendship. Barrie was fascinated by the three children: George Llewelyn Davis, age four and a half, Jack, age three, and the baby, Peter, who was one, and as he got to know them began telling them fantastic tales of adventures, princes, fairies, and pirates. When Barrie and his wife met the children's parents, Arthur and Sylvia Llewelyn Davis, daughter of George du Maurier (who wrote *Trilby*), a fast friendship began which was to last the rest of their lives. The families often spent holidays together in a country house. There Barrie would stage little plays starring both the children and the adults. One such, which Barrie called "Wendy and Peter," involved a pirate ship, a magical island, and siblings who discovered the existence of a flying boy named Peter Pan. The name Peter surely came from baby Peter Llewelyn Davis. The family dog in the play, Nana,

A CHARACTER WITH THE SAME FIRST AND LAST NAMES

Humbert Humbert
(*Lolita*)

was a double of Barrie's Newfoundland, named Luath. The play soon developed into something more serious; it was professionally produced to huge success. Barrie noted in his diary, "It is as if long after writing 'Peter Pan' its true meaning comes to me. Desperate attempts to grow up, but can't." And he wrote to the Davis children many years later saying, "I am sometimes asked who and what Peter is, but that is all he is, the spark I got from you." Although American audiences know Peter Pan's archenemy, Captain Hook, as a comic figure, he did not seem that way to the play's early audiences. Daphne du Maurier, author of *Rebecca* and daughter of the actor who originated the role of Hook, Gerald du Maurier, called him "a tragic and rather ghastly creation. . . . All boys had their Hooks; he was the phantom who came at night and stole his way into their murky dreams."

Peter Rabbit
The Tale of Peter Rabbit by Beatrix Potter (1901)

"*I* have never quite understood the secret of Peter's perennial charm," Potter wrote many years after the astounding success of her beloved bunny. "Perhaps it is because he and his little friends keep on their way; busily absorbed in their own doings." Peter was born in a letter Potter sent to her former governess's son, Noel Moore, a little boy who was very sick. "My dear Noel," she wrote, "I don't

The only emotion I have for Benjy is grief and pity for all mankind. You can't feel anything for Benjy because he doesn't feel anything.

—WILLIAM FAULKNER

know what to write to you, so I shall tell you a story about four little rabbits whose names were Flopsy, Mopsy, Cottontail, and Peter." To liven up her letter she included line drawings of each rabbit. Potter, who lived on a farm in England's Lake District, had had a rabbit named Benjamin Bounce. By 1893 she had another one, which she called Peter—whose name she borrowed for her fictional character. She continued to write letters to Noel, enlarging Peter Rabbit's world, for which she drew on her own surroundings. The shed, Mr. McGregor's garden, the byways and hedges of her animals' lives, were the vistas she saw out her own windows. After reading a number of Potter's letters Noel's mother suggested she make a book out of them. Potter embraced the idea, but found little interest from publishers. Her manuscript was rejected everywhere, literally. And so she decided to publish it herself. The rest is, of course, publishing history. Since then many a man named McGregor has been asked by small children if he was the *real* Mr. McGregor. Before she owned it, Potter rented her house from a man named McGregor, but she said she had never known anyone by that name. She was amused to note that "several bearded horticulturalists have resented the nickname."

Peter Wimsey
Whose Body? by Dorothy Sayers (1923)

*D*orothy Sayers was never able to tell her readers how and where she invented Lord Peter Wimsey, claiming memory lapse, although she complained that it was odd that a writer could never invent a name for a character which did not already exist. "My impression is that I was thinking of writing a detective story, and that he walked in, complete with spats, and applied in an airy don't-care-if-I-get-it way for the job of hero," wrote Sayers about her character, who continues to delight readers with his humor, his detecting

It would be a great joke on the people in my books if I just left them high and dry, waiting for me. If they bully me and do what they choose I have them over a barrel. They can't move until I pick up a pencil. They are frozen, turned to ice standing one foot up and with the same smile they had yesterday when I stopped.

—JOHN STEINBECK

Actors know how they end up—I mean how their
characters end up—before they speak the opening lines.
Shouldn't writers know at least as much about their
characters as actors know?

—JOHN IRVING

skills, and his highly eccentric persona. Sayers took up writing as a lark. Wimsey does seem to have leapt out at her almost full-blown, but the writing of his adventures was not easy. She did it for the money, feeling that her stories could have no literary pretensions. "Silly," she called each of Wimsey's cases; "a rather rotten story." "I hate it." But for fifteen years she carried on, earning an enormous sum from Wimsey's popularity with readers. Harriet Vane, Wimsey's female foil and eventual wife, was based largely on Sayers herself, both in looks and in personality—the emotionalism, the deep voice, the quick intelligence, the interesting but not beautiful features, were all Sayers's. Even Vane's address was set around the corner from Sayers's own house. Sayers later said she was sick of writing about Wimsey and wanted to find a way to bring him to a close. "I am getting a bit weary of Lord Peter. . . . There are times when I wish him the victim of one of his own plots!" The invention of Vane was intended to help bring the entire series to a close. Which Harriet Vane did.

Philip Marlowe
The Big Sleep by Raymond Chandler (1939)

*D*ashiell Hammett invented the hard-boiled novel, but Chandler developed it and, through his stories, created a detective figure who came to define the genre. Chandler had worked unhappily as an executive for an oil company in California. Fired at the age of fifty, he had to find work. He had written on the side for pulp magazines like *Black Mask*, and his publisher liked his stories well enough to suggest that he try something longer and more fleshed out. Drawing on some detectives he had created for his short fiction, Chandler pieced together a man he thought could sustain a longer narrative. He named him for Marlowe House, a dormitory at the school he had attended in London (a school also attended by two other creators of famous characters, P. G. Wodehouse and C. S. Forester). Marlowe, whose smoldering toughness and weary cynicism spoke to the hearts of his readers, was an instant success. Chandler only wrote five novels featuring his private eye, but he knew him as well as anyone ever knew another person. While he answered one fan to remind him that Marlowe was, after all, only a fictional character and thus could not be expected to behave like a real person, in 1951 he wrote an extraordinary letter in response to another fan letter he'd received. In it he delineated every single aspect of Marlowe's life, all of the private details, all of the physical characteristics, all of his moods and likes and dislikes. It remains the most complete picture of a fictional character ever written by its creator. Eventually Chandler grew weary of Marlowe, to whom he seemed inextricably bound. "P. Marlowe is acting up," he complained, noting that Marlowe had been too much discussed and picked over. "I'd like to forget all about Mr. Marlowe for several years." But he couldn't—he needed the income.

Princess Daisy
Princess Daisy by Judith Krantz (1978)

Judith Krantz had only just finished her first novel, *Scruples*, which was to become a huge and instant worldwide bestseller, when she began thinking about her second. An affluent woman who had grown up in comfortable circumstances and was happily married, she had done some writing for magazines and found that she loved the act of putting words to paper. One night she awoke with a single line running through her head: "She was born Princess Marguerite Alexandrovna Valensky, but everyone always called her Daisy." Turning on the light, she wrote the sentence down and taped it on the mirror in her husband's bathroom, hoping he would read it and encourage her to continue writing. Krantz later said that she has never known anyone called Daisy. But the name has popped up in several of her books. As she notes in her autobiography, once you find the right name, "it's a gift to accept without question." She finished the outline of her book about Daisy even before *Scruples* was actually published, noting in her diary how much she loved her new heroine. Another character in the book was inspired when Krantz read about Pamela Harriman, a woman who was greatly successful both as a public figure (she became the American ambassador to France) and, supposedly, with men. Krantz was told that Harriman had kept an exceptionally comfortable home. Krantz began to mull over a woman who knew how to keep a well-ordered, luxurious house—which thought led directly to Krantz's invention of the beloved mistress Annabel.

I give way to no one in my admiration for that good man [Charles Dickens]. But I think that if he had dropped all the Turveydrops and Tittletits and the other extraordinary names he gave to people, he would have made his work more realistic.

—ARTHUR CONAN DOYLE

CHARACTER OF A TEACHER WITH THE BEST NAME

Mrs. Doasyouwouldbedoneby

(in Charles Kingsley's *The Water-Babies: A Fairy Tale for a Land-Baby*)

Randall Patrick McMurphy
One Flew Over the Cuckoo's Nest by Ken Kesey (1962)

*I*n the early 1960s Kesey was a volunteer at Veteran's Hospital in Menlo Park, California. There he got paid to take part in the government's experiments with hallucinogenic drugs, including LSD, and to record what he experienced during the sessions. After the experiments were done, he stayed on at the hospital, working as a psychiatric aide on the midnight-to-eight shift. He had little to do during his shift besides mopping floors and patrolling the ward, so he began writing down the outline of a novel based on his surroundings. The patients provided the perfect characters for him; even the nurses, stiff and military, could be drawn. Kesey first wrote the book from the point of view of an aide, himself specifically. But somehow the story did not have the impact he was hoping for. He knew he needed a strong main character, a catalyst for the book's action and message. Strength, he felt, was the key. And so he resolved to try to deliberately create a character as memorable as Holden

I think most of my characters would like their actions to count for something. But at the same time they've reached the point—as so many people do—that they know it isn't so. It doesn't add up any longer.

—RAYMOND CARVER

Caulfield in *The Catcher in the Rye* or Humbert Humbert in *Lolita*, someone who jumped off the pages at the reader. McMurphy was the figure he needed, and built. Kesey later described him as "every movie show cowboy that ever walked down a main street toward the OK corral, every patriot that ever died for his country on a scaffold in history books."

Rebecca
Rebecca by Daphne du Maurier (1938)

Rebecca was the true portrait of a woman's fear. Du Maurier began her novel while traveling through Egypt. She had married a dashing military man, an officer in the Grenadier Guards. But he had been involved in a mad love affair with another woman before her, a woman who, du Maurier heard, was everything she was not: exotic, high-strung, darkly beautiful. The plain du Maurier was ravaged by jealousy and fear that her husband would never get over his first great love, Jan Ricardo. Her response was to set her fear down on paper, drawing the portrait of a man, Max de Winter, who (seemingly) could not forget his first wife. The narrator, a plain, very shy young woman beset by indecision and lack of confidence, was clearly du Maurier herself, to a T. And to all of their friends the narrator, Jan, was clearly the young Daphne du Maurier. Du Maurier's killing off of Rebecca in the novel was said to reflect how she wanted Jan to be treated. After the book was published du Maurier became embroiled in a plagiarism lawsuit. Although it had no merit and was eventually dismissed, she was terrified that she would have to testify in court to the basis for her book, thus revealing to her husband how she felt about him and Jan Ricardo.

I wonder how many times the originals of Hamlet or Tom Brown or Robinson Crusoe or Gulliver or David Copperfield or any other of the great tragic figures of history were buried and resurrected?

—MARK TWAIN

It will easily be believed that I am a fond parent to every
child of my fancy, and that no one can ever love that
family as dearly as I love them. But like many fond
parents I have in my heart of hearts a favorite child.
And his name is David Copperfield.

—CHARLES DICKENS

Reginald Wexford
From Doon with Death by Ruth Rendell (1964)

Chief Inspector Wexford, who has appeared in nearly twenty novels to date by Ruth Rendell, the great English writer of mysteries and novels of psychological suspense, came by his name in the most mundane fashion. Rendell had recently vacationed in an Irish coastal town when she began her first novel featuring a short-tempered country policeman. The town was called Wexford. Later she said, "It might easily have been Waterford." Such is the fate of fictional characters.

Roderick Alleyn
A Man Lay Dead by Ngaio Marsh (1934)

New Zealand-born Marsh was lying about her basement apartment one rainy day, idly thumbing through a detective novel. Her mother had gone to visit friends for the weekend, and she was alone. The book she was reading had potential but was ultimately unsatisfying, and Marsh felt that she could write a better book herself. So she put on her raincoat and went to the local stationery shop, where she bought paper, a pencil, and a pencil sharpener. Without further ado she began to create a hero. She wanted her detective to be an attractive man, educated and civilized, but formidable to his enemies. When she had a good idea of his nature, she named him for Roderick Alleyn, the founder of a school her father had attended, because she liked the solid Scottish name. So was born the reserved, fastidious Chief Detective-Inspector Alleyn. For each of her books after that Marsh always started by inventing her cast of characters, with Alleyn remaining the lead. She always liked her main character. "I've never gotten tired of the old boy," she said.

Rumpole
Rumpole of the Bailey by John Mortimer (1978)

*J*ohn Mortimer had had several simultaneous careers before he created the barrister Rumpole. Like his father before him, he served in London as a barrister, that is, a defending lawyer in criminal trials. While doing his legal work he had also written radio plays and several novels. In the 1970s Mortimer felt that, after a lifetime of seeing justice acted out on a daily basis, he wanted to write a detective story for his own amusement. His experiences in court provided the obvious forum. He thought of a man not unlike himself or his father, dressed him in his father's old-fashioned striped pants and wig, and sprinkled him with his father's cigar ash, creating Rumpole the barrister. Mortimer has said that some of the basis for Rumpole was an elderly barrister Mortimer came to know quite well, James Burge, who liked to call difficult judges "darling" and whose playful sense of humor could keep a court off-balance for days. Mortimer gave Rumpole his father's habit of quoting poetry at the most inappropriate times, and a powerful wife so that he would be as beset at home as he was in a court of law. Rumpole, down-at-the-heels, cunning, and courageous,

Boy, you don't have to go away from Pottsville to get people to write about. Write a piece about Squirrel Row. Get your mother to tell you the histories of the Muirs, McClures, Chambers, Althouses, McCools. Why, Faulkner never had anyone like them to write about, and they're right at your doorstep.

—JOHN O'HARA

seems to have taken on a life of his own. "I found that as soon as he stepped on the page, he began to speak in his own voice, which is undoubtedly the greatest favor a character can do for you," wrote Mortimer.

Sadie Thompson
"Rain" by Somerset Maugham (1923)

*S*omerset Maugham is perhaps best remembered for his powerful short stories, many set among the Pacific Islands at a time when the colonial powers held sway. Of these, "Rain" has remained his best-known tale: the account of a prostitute who is confronted by an overzealous missionary determined to change her ways. In the end, the missionary cuts his own throat after what the reader presumes was a sexual encounter with her. Maugham was traveling to Australia by steamer in 1916. Among his fellow passengers were a missionary couple from New England as well as a prostitute, who had been forced to leave Hawaii. Throughout the long journey the prostitute, a slatternly blonde who liked to dress in white—dress, hat, and boots—kept up a constant din from her cabin, playing music day and night and carousing. When the ship stopped in Eastern Samoa for new provisions, it was quarantined for extra inspections. The weather was ghastly—hot and humid, with a constant rain. Maugham later complained that the creaking bedsprings of

Portnoy wasn't a character for me, he was an explosion.

—PHILIP ROTH

his unsavory neighbor, gamboling with her new Samoan lover, drove him to distraction (they "created a horrid disturbance"). Maugham never spoke with her, but the visible tension between her and the missionary couple intrigued him immensely. He began to wonder what would happen if the husband, an upright and unhappy man with an exaggeratedly moralistic wife, became involved with her. Thus was born the germ of his tale of Sadie Thompson, which fueled a play and several movie versions and made Maugham's name.

Sally Bowles
Goodbye to Berlin by Christopher Isherwood (1939)

From the late 1920s to 1933 Isherwood lived in Berlin, a city he had gone to with other English writers to escape the harsh puritanical codes of post-World War I England. He went, as he said, to find boys. It was there that he found a friend who would become his most lasting literary creation—Sally Bowles, the sexually mercenary, vain, freewheeling would-be singer who was immortalized in

Cabaret, the musical version of Isherwood's story sequence *Goodbye to Berlin*. The real Sally Bowles was Jean Ross, a very young English girl who made her living off of the men she met and slept with. Ross was good-looking but not beautiful, nor was she especially sexy. But she was spunky and fun, and never felt sorry for herself. Isherwood always remembered her large brown eyes, her white face, her shiny dark hair, and her bilious green nail polish, a detail he used in his book. He liked her toughness and her jaunty, unsentimental attitude. But later in his life he found that the actresses who played her were almost more real, and more easy to remember, than the girl he had known in Berlin. Upon meeting Julie Harris, who was to star in the play version of his book, he was stunned—she was "much more like Sally than the real girl who long ago gave me the idea for my character." Ross and Isherwood were like brother and sister for a time—they shared no sexual intimacy, but came to rely on each other in a city and world that were becoming increasingly dangerous politically. Although they separated after just a few months, once the Nazis had fully taken over Berlin, they remained faithful correspondents until Ross's death in 1973.

*N*athan Zuckerman is an act. It's all the art of impersonation, isn't it? That's the fundamental novelistic gift.

—PHILIP ROTH

Sam Spade

The Maltese Falcon by Dashiell Hammett
(1930)

*R*aymond Chandler once said, "Hammett took murder out of the Venetian vase and dropped it in the alley." And *The Maltese Falcon* was the book that did so. Perhaps no other mystery novel has been so imitated, so admired, so iconified. Hammett's cast of characters was unusual but completely believable, and his private eye, Sam Spade, became the emblem of the tough guy who's on the right side of the law—at the end. After his stint as a detective for the Pinkerton Agency, chronic illness caused Hammett to turn to writing for a living. He could no longer hold down a full-time job. He published pulp stories and several novels before introducing Spade to the world. In creating him, he gave his hero his own real first name, which he never used—Samuel. But beyond that he had no specific model in mind for the ultimate gumshoe, although he did base the character of Cairo on a man he picked up on a forgery charge, and Casper Gutman, the fat man made famous by Sydney Greenstreet in the movie version of the book, came from a fat man Hammett had once followed, suspecting he was a German secret agent. He was often asked who had provided the template for Spade. Hammett replied that Spade was "a dream man," that is, the kind of man most real detectives would have liked to be. Tough, versatile, sexy, bordering on amoral, Spade represented the ideal version of these men's lives, as they saw it.

Santiago
The Old Man and the Sea by Ernest Hemingway (1952)

*T*he novella that would win Hemingway the Pulitzer Prize for fiction was written in Cuba at Hemingway's house, Finca Vigía. It was originally intended to be part of a larger work, an ambitious three-part novel Hemingway referred to as "the Sea Book." The first part, which was specifically set at sea and was to feature an old man fighting the forces of nature, was to be called "The Sea in Being," or, later, "The Dignity of Man." Hemingway never completed his big book, and it was left to the executors of his estate to issue another part of this work as the posthumously published *Islands in the Stream*. The Sea Book was germinated by several events: one was an incident Hemingway witnessed while out in his boat, the *Pilar*. One day Hemingway and the *Pilar*'s skipper saw an old man and a young boy in a small boat being pulled furiously forward by a huge fish they had hooked. Hemingway offered to help, but was

Q: *Where do you get your characters?*
Kurt Vonnegut: Cincinnati.

angrily waved off. The old man clearly intended to land the fish himself. For the better part of the afternoon Hemingway watched the titanic struggle; every attempt he made to help, or to offer water, was rebuffed. Much earlier, in the 1930s, Hemingway had been told about a local legend involving an old man who had hooked a massive marlin. The man was pulled far out to sea; when he was rescued days later, only the skeleton of the fish remained, lashed to the side of the tiny fishing boat. Hemingway wrote this up for *Esquire* as local Cuban legend. Later, he turned these two incidents into his tale, which a few critics snidely called "the poor man's *Moby-Dick*."

Scarlett O'Hara

Gone with the Wind by Margaret Mitchell (1936)

*J*n 1927, while laid up after a minor car accident, Margaret Mitchell read through all the books available in her local library. One day her husband came home with a box of blank paper, and gave it to her, suggesting that she write a good book if she wanted something new to read. Mitchell had long been interested in the history of her native

Georgia, and so she began, writing out on a piece of paper, "She had never understood either of the men she loved and so she lost them both." Mitchell's novel grew longer and longer, and encompassed the entire Civil War. To flesh out her characters she used people she knew, starting with the main character, a feisty, headstrong young woman she named Pansy O'Hara. Pansy was very much the image of her creator, and shared many traits and life events with her. The public never knew how many of the violent events in Pansy's life were mirrors of Mitchell's own personal tragedies. She even had Pansy's love life recreate her own: engagement to a weak-seeming man who died in battle—Ashley Wilkes in the novel, Clifford Henry in Mitchell's life; and marriage to a very physical, powerful, somewhat scandalous man—Rhett Butler in the novel, Red Upshaw, her first husband, in real life. So close were the parallels that when Upshaw, whom she had divorced, read the finished novel, he recognized himself in Rhett Butler and called

SOME ORPHANED CHARACTERS

Oliver Twist (*Oliver Twist*)

Sara Crewe
(*A Little Princess*)

Mary Lennox
(*The Secret Garden*)

Harry Potter
(the Harry Potter novels)

Heidi (*Heidi*)

Huckleberry Finn
(*The Adventures of Huckleberry Finn*)

Mitchell to proclaim that she clearly still loved him. Mitchell also used some of her grandmother's experiences as fodder for Pansy's actions, such as helping put out the fires in Atlanta during the great burning of the city, or nursing wounded soldiers, or fighting off carpetbaggers. Rhett Butler's name was a clear melding of two old Southern family names. But Pansy was problematic. When the novel was eventually accepted for publication, her editor in New York suggested that the word "pansy" might make for unhappy associations. Mitchell, not quite grasping the point, then suggested her heroine be named Nancy, or Peggy (her own nickname). Finally she found Scarlett in the book itself, in a reference to an ancestral family of the fictional Fitzgeralds, and Scarlett stuck. The plantation Tara was a new invention as well; Mitchell had written the book using the fictional name Fontenoy Hall. The book went on to win the Pulitzer

The Lion, the Witch and the Wardrobe *all began with a picture of a Faun carrying an umbrella and parcels in a snowy wood. This picture had been in my mind since I was about sixteen. Then one day, when I was about forty, I said to myself, "Let's try to make a story about it."*

—C. S. LEWIS

*There is no such thing as a "minor"
character in Dostoevski.*

—F. SCOTT FITZGERALD

Prize and has remained a constant best-seller since it was first published.

Sherlock Holmes
A Study in Scarlet by Arthur Conan Doyle (1886)

Would the great Sherlock Holmes be as memorable if Conan Doyle had kept to one of his original names for the detective: Sheridan Hope, or Sherrinford Holmes? Conan Doyle had a small medical practice when he began writing the series of detective stories that would immortalize him. He had dabbled in writing stories, but nothing really stuck. Then he remembered his years as a medical student in Edinburgh. His teacher there, a surgeon, was Dr. Joseph Bell, author of a renowned manual of surgical operations and by all accounts a brilliant teacher. Bell was tall and very thin with a sharp profile and gray eyes. His talks were brilliant, punctuated by extraordinary moments of discovery. Bell liked to approach people and, at a glance, tell them things about their work, their personal lives, their habits, that were astounding in their accuracy. But how could he know such things? Conan Doyle and his fellow medical students were amazed. Years later Conan Doyle recalled his teacher and put him on paper as his detective who uses similar methods to pull together facts. After Holmes's success (which did not come quickly—the first book was rejected by several publishers) Conan Doyle wrote to Bell, "It is most certainly to you that I owe Sherlock Holmes." The name Holmes is thought to have come from Conan Doyle's great admiration for the American physician and writer Oliver Wendell Holmes, author of *The Autocrat of the Breakfast Table,* who was in the middle of a public speaking tour of England at the time Conan Doyle began writing the Sherlock Holmes stories. And he had known several Dr. Watsons, including one who was an assistant to Dr. Bell (although at first he called Holmes's faithful friend Ormond Sackler). In later years Holmes's phenomenal success grated on Conan Doyle, who had grown sick of the endless demand for more adventures. He tried to kill him off in 1893—"I am weary of his name," he wrote his mother. And in a speech he said, "I have had

M*y heroine is what the flapper would like to* think *she is—the actual flapper is a much duller and grayer proposition. I tried to set down different aspects of an individual—I was accused of creating a type.*

—F. SCOTT FITZGERALD

such an overdose of him. . . . [I]t was not murder but justifiable homicide in self-defense, since if I had not killed him, he would certainly have killed me." But Conan Doyle was stunned by the public's hostile, even violent response. He realized he had made such an impression on contemporary readers that he simply had to continue. And so Holmes was resurrected, to continue until Conan Doyle's death.

Sophie
Sophie's Choice by William Styron (1976)

$\mathcal{O}$n returning home to the United States from his stint as a marine in World War II, William Styron, a Southerner, moved to New York City, where he hoped to become a writer. He found a rooming house in Brooklyn, at 1506 Caton Avenue, that seemed congenial, but—in one version of the genesis of Sophie—before long his concentration was interrupted by a very active couple living just above him; their lovemaking was loud and seemingly constant, and even shook his light fixtures. One resident of "the Pink Palace," as Styron called his building, was a pleasant young blonde who had managed to survive the Auschwitz death camp. A Polish Catholic, she turned out to be one of the noisy lovers who kept him from his work. Her name was Sophie. "She was a young woman who disappeared from my life almost as quickly as she came," recalled Styron. But the impression she

Show me a hero and I will write you a tragedy.

—F. SCOTT FITZGERALD

made on him stayed for years. Much later, in 1974, in the midst of trying to write a book about the Marine Corps—and getting nowhere with it—he suddenly remembered her, and his life in Brooklyn, as he awoke from a nap. He had a conscious vision and memory of Sophie "looking very beautiful in the middle of summer with a sort of summer dress on and her arm bared and the tattoo visible." He immediately set to work, blending the real Sophie with another woman he had heard of, who had had to choose between her children at a death camp during the war, and wrote out what became *Sophie's Choice*, hardly pausing for breaks.

Stuart Little
Stuart Little by E. B. White (1939)

*U*nlike *Charlotte's Web*, for which White studied spiders and which he planned as a children's book from the beginning, *Stuart Little* was not intended to be a book. One morning White awoke from a dream in which a little mouse appeared fully dressed. The creature had a hat and carried a cane and was fully formed. White felt he had been given a gift—and that to change the mouse into something else, say, a grasshopper, would be untrue to his dream. Over the next twelve years White fitfully wrote the tale of Stuart Little, reading each episode aloud to young relatives. Only gradually did it come together as a united narrative, one that became, as White noted, "the story of a quest—the quest for beauty."

Tess Durbeyfield
Tess of the d'Urbervilles by Thomas Hardy (1891)

*H*ardy often said that his story of a family that had once seen grander days, and of a young woman caught by a tragic love, was based on fact. One source may have been a maid, Jenny Phillips, who worked for Hardy's family and who had an illegitimate child who died a few days after his birth (like Tess's). Another source often mentioned is Hardy's own mother, who was a dairymaid on an estate.

The term "creation of character" (or characters) is misleading. Characters pre-exist. They are found. *They reveal themselves slowly to the novelist's perception—as might fellow-travellers seated opposite one in a very dimly-lit railway carriage.*

—ELIZABETH BOWEN

"Tess's life and adventures and final death are practically what happened to a relative of ours," a cousin of Hardy said. And Hardy told his publisher that if it had not been too personal, he could have called the novel *Tess of the Hardys*. His heroine went through several name changes, as did the book. She was called Sue (and the book *The Body and Soul of Sue*) and Rose Mary and Love (when the book was *Too Late, Beloved!*).

Tom Ripley
The Talented Mr. Ripley by Patricia Highsmith (1955)

*T*exas-born Highsmith had written one novel before she created Ripley: the chilling story of arranged murder *Strangers on a Train*, which became one of Alfred Hitchcock's greatest films. One morning, very early, Highsmith was walking on a beach in Positano, Italy, when she saw a lonely-looking young man walking by himself. She

N.B.—the unanswerability of the question, from an outsider: "Are the characters in your novel invented, or are they from real life?" Obviously, neither is true. The outsider's notion of "real life" and the novelist's are hopelessly apart.

—ELIZABETH BOWEN

*The one time I met William Faulkner, I asked him how
he had come to imagine his truculent black character
Lucas Beauchamp. "I saw him," answered Faulkner,
"walking across my typewriter."*

—IRVING HOWE

began to wonder what he was doing there and why he was alone. She went back to her room and began to play with the idea. The novel flowed swiftly. "I often had the feeling Ripley was writing and I was typing," she recalled. Highsmith correctly noted that it is not necessary for the reader to like a book's hero as long as the story is entertaining. Even if the hero is evil, it is the writer's duty to "have a frolic" with the hero's psychological makeup. Indeed, Tom Ripley commits at least a dozen murders in the novels that feature him, yet he is without a doubt one of the most likable hero/villains in modern fiction.

Tom Sawyer
Tom Sawyer by Mark Twain (1876)

Huck Finn was based directly on a real boy Twain knew in Hannibal, Missouri. Tom Sawyer, though, was not one single figure. His was an ordinary name that "seemed to fit the boy." Who was the real boy? Twain was asked. "Town's full of 'em." Twain combined two school-yard friends with his own adventures as a boy, turning his character into "the composite order of architecture."

Travis McGee
The Deep Blue Goodbye
by John D. MacDonald (1964)

*M*acDonald had often been ill as a child. Confined to his bed, he read voraciously, loving especially the works of Robert Louis Stevenson among other adventure writers. During World War II he had sent his wife stories from the war zone in place of standard letters. She liked them so much she sent them on to the pulp magazines that were so popular at the time—and they were accepted. His career as a writer had begun. He had written and published more than two hundred novels in this way when his editor asked him to think about starting a series which could be extended indefinitely. Initially MacDonald didn't like the idea, feeling that if he created a successful series he would be stuck with it, and bound to it, for the rest of his writing life—which proved all too true. But his editor persisted, and wanting to break out of his current writing track, MacDonald agreed. The series would be linked, they decided, and identifiable to readers, through some common element. Gemstones, perhaps, or months of the year. At lunch in a New York restaurant called the Red Devil they hit on the use of colors—each new book would have a different color in the title. MacDonald then decided to create a lone figure who was on the side of the law yet who used sometimes unscrupulous means to achieve good. MacDonald had a friend named Dallas, whose name he appropriated for his hero, saying later that "geographic names are fun, and easy to remember, like Tennessee Williams." And he set him in Florida, where MacDonald himself lived—but in Fort Lauderdale, on the east coast of the state and far away from MacDonald's home in Sarasota. MacDonald had a strange hunch that if his series became popular, McGee's hometown would be overrun by droves of tourists and autograph seekers. In 1963 MacDonald wrote no less than four books featuring Dallas McGee, each of which was to be published the following year separated by a few months. Then tragedy struck in Dallas, Texas, on

SOME EPONYMOUS TITLES

Rebecca

Justine

Martin Chuzzlewit

Mr. Roberts

Mrs. Dalloway

Myra Breckenridge

Lolita

Elmer Gantry

Oliver Twist

Mrs. Bridge

Barry Lyndon

Pal Joey

Eugene Onegin

Gigi

The Talented Mr. Ripley

I really don't know where I get all these rascals in my book. I have certainly never lived *with such people.*

—WILLIAM THACKERAY

November 22, 1963. With the assassination of President John F. Kennedy, MacDonald realized that the name Dallas would always be synonymous with that death. But what could the new name be? MacDonald was stumped until someone suggested he look at the names of Air Force bases to find an evocative name. He did, and settled on California's Travis Air Force Base. Travis McGee went through some permutations; in MacDonald's first draft he was a somber figure, too gloomy by far. A second attempt turned him into such a glib and merry prankster that his creator couldn't stand him. A third draft settled halfway between the two extremes, to give us the Travis McGee readers have come to know and love over the course of twenty-one books.

Tristram Shandy
The Life and Opinions of Tristram Shandy, Gentleman by Laurence Sterne (1759)

*R*eaders of this serialized novel, which was published over the course of several years, were stunned and outraged to discover that Tristram Shandy, the hero, so called, of Sterne's completely original and unclassifiable tale, would remain an embryo throughout the book. This innovation caused "a terrible fermentation" in London, a city not easily shocked in the eighteenth century. To make matters worse, Sterne included immediately recognizable friends and rivals as buffoonish characters in the story. They all complained vigorously as the serializations appeared; to each complaint Sterne answered, "Sir, I have not hurt you;

A character suffers from the fear that he will become boring to the author, who will simply let him drop, without so much as a terminal illness or a dramatic tumble down the Reichenbach Falls in the arms of Professor Moriarty. For some years now, Bech had felt his author wanting to set him aside, to get him off the desk forever. Rather frantically hoping still to amuse, Bech had developed a new set of tricks, somewhat out of character—he had married, he had written a bestseller. Nevertheless, and especially as his sixties settled on him, as cumbersomely as an astronaut's suit, he felt boredom weighing from above. . . .

—JOHN UPDIKE

but take care: I am not born yet; but heaven knows what I may do in the next two volumes." "Shan" or "shandy" was a Yorkshire term meaning unsteady, or addled. After his novel was published Sterne liked to sign his letters "Shandy," delighting in annoying literary London by reminding everyone of the life of his outrageous hero. Once, at a party at the painter Sir Joshua Reynolds's house, Sterne met, for the only time in his life, the great choleric lexicographer Samuel Johnson. So much did Sterne tout the name and character of Shandy that Johnson later recalled, "In a company where I lately was, Tristram Shandy introduced himself; and Tristram Shandy had scarcely sat down, when he instructed us that he had been writing a Dedication to Lord Spencer; and *sponte sua,* for nobody desired him, he began to read it; and before he had read half a dozen lines, *sponte sua,* I told him it was not English, Sir."

*Sammy [Glick] was composed in the manner
of all fictional characters, out of the writer's
recognition of similar and overlapping traits
in various individuals who have passed
within his circle of observation.*

—BUDD SCHULBERG

I cannot tear myself away from living creatures
to bother about imaginary ones.

—LEO TOLSTOY

Walter Mitty
"The Secret Life of Walter Mitty" by James Thurber (1939)

*T*he story that introduced Walter Mitty to the world, and that showcased one of the most enduring fictional characters ever invented, begins as Mitty is driving his wife to the hairdresser's in Waterbury, Connecticut. Thurber once said that when he was on his deathbed, his wife Helen would be sure to be found at the hairdresser's. Eerily, that proved to be the case—on November 2, 1961, Mrs. Thurber was indeed at the hairdresser's when the call came that Thurber was dying. Mitty caused a sensation when he was first published. American soldiers embraced him during World War II; they imitated the "ta-pocketa-pocketa" sound Mitty would make as he imagined himself shooting guns while fighting off enemy armies, and formed Walter Mitty clubs everywhere. Mitty, a romantic daydreamer whose heroic measures in his fantasy life helped balance his weak, ineffectual real life, had no direct progenitor. While many of Thurber's friends and colleagues noted a strong similarity between the writer and his creation, Thurber himself noted

*A*fter reading The Maltese Falcon, *I went mooning*
about in a daze of love such as I had not known for
any character in literature since I encountered Sir
Lancelot at the age of nine. He is so hard-boiled you
could roll him across the White House lawn.

—DOROTHY PARKER

that Mitty was based on every man he'd ever known, imply-
ing that Mitty's situation—that of oppressed husband bat-
tling helplessly against a formidable wife—was universal.
Mrs. Thurber greatly disliked being compared to Mrs. Mitty,
or to any Thurber female character. "Of course, I am not
anything like that Mrs. Mitty," she once wrote to a librarian.
But she did make Thurber revise parts of his story, taking
out a fight Thurber had written featuring Mitty against
Ernest Hemingway at New York's Stork Club (she feared
Hemingway's temper).

Willie Stark
All the King's Men by Robert Penn Warren (1946)

*W*inner of the Pulitzer Prize for fiction, Warren's now
classic novel of American politics and corruption is
often read as a fictional biography of the legendary

Louisiana governor and senator Huey Long. For much of his life, after writing the novel, Warren protested this identification. Long did provide inspiration: "I can only be sure," Warren said, "that if I had never gone to live in Louisiana and if Huey Long had not existed, the novel would never have been written." Warren taught literature at Louisiana State University, and the oversized aura of Huey Long and the Long family cast a long shadow, even after Long's assassination in 1935. But Stark, who in the novel is a raging populist of low personal morals, a deeply corrupt politician, was

> **MORE EPONYMOUS TITLES**
>
> *Barnaby Rudge*
>
> *McTeague*
>
> *Moby-Dick*
>
> *Emma*
>
> *"Daisy Miller"*
>
> *Maurice*
>
> *Pinocchio*
>
> *Herzog*
>
> *Eugénie Grandet*
>
> *Madeline*
>
> *Black Beauty*
>
> *Mary Poppins*

truly a fictional creation. "For better or worse," said Warren, "Willie Stark was not Huey Long. Willie was only himself, whatever that self turned out to be, a shadowy wraith or a blundering human being." So realistic was Warren's creation that his readership was convinced Long was his model. Indeed, his publisher toned down some of Warren's passages for fear of offending the Long family and risking a lawsuit. But Warren, contemplating Long's death, claimed that to create Stark he drew more on Julius Caesar than on Long, and even used as a model the philosopher William James, whose pragmatic approach to life fueled Stark's approach to the people who got in his way. William Faulkner appreciated Warren's book but sniped that "Stark and the rest of them are second-rate." The public disagreed, and his novel continues to be taught in schools and colleges as the best political novel ever written.

Winnie-the-Pooh
Winnie-the-Pooh by A. A. Milne (1926)

*E*nglish author Alan Alexander Milne had written several novels (now forgotten) before turning to the children's books that would make him famous. The inspiration for his greatest creation, a small toy bear, came via his son, Christopher Robin Milne. To please his son, Milne wrote a story about his bear Pooh, and Pooh's friendship with a small boy named Christopher Robin (who in the accompanying illus-

I read some more Proust. How thoroughly he embalms his thoughts and people—not a sentence or character escapes without wax flowers on its chest and a sickening funeral smell.

—DAWN POWELL

I was sitting one morning at work upon [The Last Chronicle of Barset] at the end of the long drawing-room of the Atheneum Club,—as was then my wont when I had slept the previous night in London. As I was there, two clergymen, each with a magazine in his hand, seated themselves, one on one side of the fire and one on the other, close to me. They soon began to abuse what they were reading, and each was reading some part of some novel of mine. The gravamen of their complaint lay in the fact that I reintroduced the same characters so often! "Here," said one, "is that archdeacon whom we have had in every novel he has ever written." "And here," said the other, "is the old duke whom he has talked about till everybody is tired of him. If I could not invent new characters, I would not write novels at all." Then one of them fell foul of Mrs. Proudie. It was impossible for me not to hear their words, and almost impossible to hear them and be quiet. I got up, and standing between them, I acknowledged myself to be the culprit. "As to Mrs. Proudie," I said, "I will go home and kill her before the week is over." And so I did.

—ANTHONY TROLLOPE

When I read that great novelists like Dickens and
Trollope "killed off" a character, or changed the
conclusion of a tale, I am dumbfounded. What then was
their own relationship to their subject? But to show how
mysterious and incalculable the whole business is, one has
only to remember that Trollope "went home and killed"
Mrs. Proudie because he had heard some fool at his club
complaining that she had lived long enough; and yet that
death scene thus arbitrarily brought about is one of the
greatest pages he ever wrote. . . .

—EDITH WHARTON

trations even wore the same clothes as the real boy). "Every child has his favorite toy, and every only child has a special need for one," Christopher Robin wrote as an adult. "Pooh was mine." A small collection of stuffed animals surrounded the boy in his room: Pooh, who by the time the stories were written had lost the firmness in his stuffed neck, causing his head to flop very engagingly; and Piglet, a gift from a neighbor; and Kanga and Tigger, who were presented by his parents partly as toys and partly to add to the literary possibilities of this menagerie. As Christopher Robin noted, "Their characters were theirs from birth." Only Owl and

Rabbit were pure inventions. For the rest of his life, Christopher Robin Milne would be identified with his father's writing. He was asked for autographs and even in his old age was regarded as a small, inquisitive boy with a fabulous universe of imaginary friends. A bookseller by trade, Milne apparently never overcame the burden of the public's identification with his father's portrayal. He said that a great and tragic difference exists between an author and a book's character, for while the author will always be the author, a character, if based on real life, grows up and out of his part.

Yossarian
Catch-22 by Joseph Heller (1961)

*J*oseph Heller was a thirty-eight-year-old advertising executive for *McCall's* magazine when he wrote the book whose title would become a catchphrase of its own, a novel that became an icon for an antiwar generation.

The artist who really loves people loves them so well the way they are he sees no need to disguise their characteristics—he loves them whole, without retouching. Yet the word always used for this unqualifying affection is "cynicism."

—DAWN POWELL

Once I was able to look beyond myself, the world seemed full of characters. It's easy to disguise them enough for the purposes of putting them in a novel—just add a moustache, or change their sex, or move them to Arizona. You can do anything you want as long as you keep the essential quality that sparked your imagination in the first place. They'll never know. Trust me.

—LEE SMITH

Heller's genius was to pinpoint the essential madness of war in two words: *Catch-22*. Catch-22 was a clause stating that any soldier who was crazy could be exempted from combat duty. But to be exempted, a soldier has to ask to be exempted. And if a soldier asks to be exempted, he is clearly not crazy, since combat duty is madness. When, during World War II, Heller served in the Army Air Corps as a wing bombardier and was stationed in Corsica, a soldier named Francis Yohannon bunked in a tent nearby. Heller used a variant of his name, John Yossarian, and later said that Yossarian's fictional character was "an incarnation of a wish." His first name is never used, but Heller loved the idea that Yossarian would have a name like John, which he thought had a passive ring to it completely the opposite of Yossarian's character. He said later that if Yossarian had been English, his name would have been Charlie. Other characters came from the same group. Hungry Joe was based on a pilot, Joe Chrenko, in Heller's tent. Major————de Coverley was based on a Major Cover, the squadron's executive officer. But everyone was somewhat altered. As Heller noted, "They're products of an imagination that drew on American life in the postwar period. The Cold War, really." *Catch-22* was not a success when it was published. It was not a best-seller and won no prizes. And the review attention was mostly negative. For example, *The New Yorker* wrote that "it gives the impression of having been shouted onto paper." Today it is considered the most significant book to have come out of World War II.

A NOTE ON SOURCES

This is not meant to be a scholarly book; it is hoped that what lies between these covers will entertain and, in some cases, amuse the casual reader interested in fiction, in writers, and in literary history. To find the stories behind the famous fictional characters in this book I have scoured biographies, memoirs, diaries, collections of letters, newspapers, anecdotal accounts, and magazines, and have spoken with some of the authors included here. I have not weighted down my short anecdotes with footnotes, which would clutter and pomposify a small book of this sort, but my published sources, where attributable, are listed below.

In some biographies about the same writer, material about the origin of a writer's literary character(s), if it exists, is duplicated, more or less, in other biographies; in other instances there are divergent accounts of a writer's creative thinking. In these latter cases I have followed what seemed to me, when it comes to reading, the most likely possibility. If you read on into the literature, you will feel free to make your own judgments.

Ackroyd, Peter. *Dickens.* New York: HarperCollins, 1990.
Amis, Kingsley. *The James Bond Dossier.* New York: New American Library, 1965.

———. *Memoirs.* New York: Summit Books, 1991.

Aronoff, Myron J. *The Spy Novels of John le Carré: Balancing Ethics and Politics.* New York: St. Martin's Press, 1999.

Assouline, Pierre. *Simenon: A Biography.* New York: Alfred A. Knopf, 1997.

Bair, Deirdre. *Samuel Beckett.* New York: Summit Books, 1990.

Beahm, George, ed. *The Stephen King Companion.* Kansas City: Andrews & McMeel, 1989.

Bell, Ian. *Dreams of Exile: Robert Louis Stevenson: A Biography.* New York: Henry Holt, 1992.

Bemelmans, Ludwig. *Mad About Madeline.* New York: Viking, 1993.

Bernard, André. *Now All We Need Is a Title: Famous Book Titles and How They Got That Way.* New York: W. W. Norton, 1994.

Birkin, Andrew. *J. M. Barrie & The Lost Boys: The Love Story That Gave Birth to Peter Pan.* New York: Clarkson N. Potter, 1979.

Bloom, Harold, ed. *Brett Ashley.* New York: Chelsea House Publishers, 1991.

Brabazon, James. *Dorothy L. Sayers: A Biography.* New York: Charles Scribner's Sons, 1981.

Brenner, Gerry. *The Old Man and the Sea: Story of a Common Man.* New York: Twayne Publishers, 1991.

Bruccoli, Matthew J. *Some Sort of Epic Grandeur: The Life of F. Scott Fitzgerald.* New York: Harcourt Brace Jovanovich, 1981.

Calder, Jenni. *Robert Louis Stevenson: A Life Study.* New York: Oxford University Press, 1980.

Carpenter, Humphrey. *Tolkien: A Biography.* Boston: Houghton Mifflin, 1977.

Cate, Curtis. *Antoine de Saint-Exupéry.* New York: G. P. Putnam's Sons, 1970.

Christie, Agatha. *Agatha Christie: An Autobiography.* New York: Dodd, Mead, 1977.

Clarke, Gerald. *Capote: A Biography.* New York: Simon & Schuster, 1988.

Cohen, Morton N. *Lewis Carroll: A Biography.* New York: Alfred A. Knopf, 1995.

Colvin, Sidney, ed. *The Letters of Robert Louis Stevenson.* New York: Charles Scribner's Sons, 1924.

Cronin, Anthony. *Samuel Beckett: The Last Modernist.* New York: Harper-Collins, 1996.

Denyer, Susan. *At Home with Beatrix Potter: The Creator of Peter Rabbit.* New York: Harry N. Abrams, 2000.

DuBose, Martha Hailey. *Women of Mystery: The Lives and Works of Notable Women Crime Novelists.* New York: St. Martin's Press, 2000.

Dunbar, Janet. *J. M. Barrie: The Man Behind the Image.* Boston: Houghton Mifflin, 1970.

Eames, Hugh. *Sleuths, Inc.* Philadelphia: J. B. Lippincott, 1978.

Edwards, Anne. *The Road to Tara: The Life of Margaret Mitchell.* New York: Ticknor & Fields, 1983.

Elledge, Scott, ed. *Tess of the d'Urbervilles: A Norton Critical Edition.* New York: W. W. Norton, 1991.

Ellman, Richard. *Oscar Wilde.* New York: Alfred A. Knopf, 1988.

Forester, C. S. *Long Before Forty.* Boston: Little, Brown, 1967.

Foster, Margaret. *Daphne du Maurier: The Secret Life of the Renowned Story-teller.* New York: Doubleday, 1993.

Fugate, Francis L., and Roberta B. Fugate. *Secrets of the World's Best-Selling Writer: The Storytelling Techniques of Erle Stanley Gardner.* New York: William Morrow, 1980.

Gittings, Robert. *Thomas Hardy's Later Years.* Boston: Atlantic Monthly Press/Little, Brown, 1978.

Glossbrenner, Alfred, and Emily Glossbrenner, eds. *About the Author.* New York: Harvest Books, 2000.

Gross, Seymour, and Scully Bradley, Richmond Croom-Beatty, and E. Hudson Lang, eds. *The Scarlet Letter: A Norton Critical Edition.* New York: W. W. Norton, 1988.

Guth, Dorothy Lobrano, ed. *The Letters of E. B. White.* New York: Harper & Row, 1976.

Hearn, Michael Patrick, ed. *The Annotated Huckleberry Finn.* New York: W. W. Norton, 2001.

Heller, Joseph. *Now and Then: From Coney Island to Here.* New York: Alfred A. Knopf, 1998.

Hemmings, F. W. J. *Alexandre Dumas: The King of Romance.* New York: Charles Scribner's Sons, 1979.

Hillerman, Tony. *Seldom Disappointed: A Memoir.* New York: HarperCollins, 2001.

Holmes, Charles S. *The Clocks of Columbus: The Literary Career of James Thurber.* New York: Atheneum, 1972.

Holmes, Richard. *Shelley: The Pursuit.* New York: E. P. Dutton, 1975.

Honberger, Eric. *John le Carré.* London: Methuen, 1986.

Hughes, Dorothy. *Erle Stanley Gardner: The Case of the Real Perry Mason: A Biography.* New York: William Morrow, 1978.

Isherwood, Christopher. *The Berlin Stories.* New York: New Directions, 1963.
———. *Christopher and His Kind: 1929–1939.* New York: Farrar, Straus & Giroux, 1976.

Jacobs, Eric. *Kingsley Amis: A Biography.* New York: St. Martin's Press, 1998.

James, P. D. *Time to Be in Earnest: A Fragment of Autobiography.* New York: Alfred A. Knopf, 2000.

Kaplan, Justin. *Mr. Clemens and Mark Twain: A Biography.* New York: Simon & Schuster, 1966.

Kinney, Harrison. *James Thurber: His Life and Times.* New York: Henry Holt, 1995.

Knowles, Owen, and Gene Moore. *The Oxford Reader's Companion to Conrad.* New York: Oxford University Press, 2000.

Krantz, Judith. *Sex and Shopping: The Confessions of a Nice Jewish Girl.* New York: St. Martin's Press, 2000.

Kuehl, John, and Jackson Breyer, eds. *Dear Scott, Dear Max: The Fitzgerald-Perkins Correspondence.* New York: Charles Scribner's Sons, 1971.

Lauer, Kristin O., and Cynthia Griffin Wolff, eds. *Ethan Frome: A Norton Critical Edition.* New York: W. W. Norton, 1995.

Lewis, Margaret. *Ngaio Marsh: A Life.* New York: Poisoned Pen Press, 1991.

Linder, Leslie. *A History of the Writings of Beatrix Potter.* London: Frederick
    Warne, 1971.

Lodge, David. *The Art of Fiction.* New York: Viking Press, 1992.

————. *The Practice of Writing.* New York: Penguin Books, 1996.

MacShane, Frank, ed. *Selected Letters of Raymond Chandler.* New York:
    Columbia University Press, 1981.

Marnham, Patrick. *The Man Who Wasn't Maigret: A Portrait of Georges
    Simenon.* New York: Farrar, Straus & Giroux, 1993.

Martin, Jay. *Nathanael West: The Art of His Life.* New York: Farrar, Straus &
    Giroux, 1970.

Maugham, W. Somerset. *The Art of Fiction.* New York: Doubleday, 1955.

Maurois, François. *Alexandre Dumas.* New York: Alfred A. Knopf, 1966.

McAleer, John. *Rex Stout: A Biography.* New York: Little, Brown, 1977.

McLynn, Frank. *Robert Louis Stevenson.* New York: Random House, 1993.

McNally, Raymond T., and Radu Florescu. *In Search of Dracula: The History of
    Dracula and Vampires.* Boston: Houghton Mifflin, 1994.

Melrose, A. R., ed. *Beyond the World of Pooh: Selections from the Memoirs of
    Christopher Milne.* New York: Dutton, 1998.

Merrill, Hugh. *The Red Hot Typewriter.* New York: St. Martin's Press, 2000.

Meyers, Eric. *Uncle Mame: The Life of Patrick Dennis.* New York: St. Martin's
    Press, 2000.

Meyers, Jeffrey. *Joseph Conrad: A Biography.* New York: Charles Scribner's
    Sons, 1991.

Miller, Edwin Haviland. *Salem Is My Dwelling Place: A Life of Nathaniel
    Hawthorne.* Iowa City: University of Iowa Press, 1991.

Millgate, Michael. *Thomas Hardy: A Biography.* New York: Random House,
    1982.

Monaghan, David. *The Novels of John le Carré.* New York: Basil Blackwell, 1985.

Morgan, Ted. *Maugham.* New York: Simon & Schuster, 1980.

Mortimer, John. *Murderers and Other Friends: Another Part of Life.* New York:
    Viking Press, 1994.

Neider, Charles, ed. *The Autobiography of Mark Twain*. New York: Harper & Brothers, 1959.

Nolan, William F. *Hammett: A Life at the Edge*. New York: Congdon & Weed, 1983.

Osborne, Charles, ed. *The Bram Stoker Bedside Companion*. New York: Taplinger, 1979.

Parker, Hershel, and Harrison Hayford, eds. *Moby-Dick: A Norton Critical Edition*. New York: W. W. Norton, 2002.

Pevear, Richard, and Larissa Volokhonsky, trans. *Anna Karenina*. New York: Viking, 2001.

Plimpton, George, ed. *Truman Capote: In Which Various Friends, Enemies, Acquaintances and Detractors Recall His Turbulent Career*. New York: Doubleday, 1997.

———. *Writers at Work: The Paris Review Interviews I–VII*. New York: Viking Press, 1996.

Reynolds, Barbara. *Dorothy Sayers: Her Life and Soul*. New York: St. Martin's Press, 1993.

———, ed. *The Letters of Dorothy L. Sayers*. New York: St. Martin's Press, 1975.

Reynolds, Michael. *Hemingway: The Paris Years*. New York: W. W. Norton, 1989.

Salzman, Jack, and Pamela Wilkinson, eds. *Major Characters in American Fiction*. New York: Henry Holt, 1994.

Schiff, Stacy. *Saint-Exupéry: A Biography*. New York: Alfred A. Knopf, 1994.

Schmidgall, Gary. *The Stranger Wilde: Interpreting Oscar*. New York: Dutton, 1994.

Seymour-Smith, Martin. *Hardy: A Biography*. New York: St. Martin's Press, 1994.

Sorkin, Adam J., ed. *Conversations with Joseph Heller*. Jackson: University Press of Mississippi, 1993.

Stashower, Daniel. *Teller of Tales: The Life of Arthur Conan Doyle.* New York: Henry Holt, 1999.

Steegmuller, Francis. *Flaubert in Egypt.* Boston: Atlantic Monthly Press, 1974.

Symons, Julian. *Dashiell Hammett.* New York: Harcourt Brace Jovanovich, 1985.

Tanner, Stephen L. *Ken Kesey.* Boston: Twayne Publishers, 1983.

Tennant, Roger. *Joseph Conrad.* New York: Atheneum, 1981.

Trollope, Anthony. *An Autobiography.* New York: Oxford University Press, 1950.

Troyat, Henri. *Tolstoy.* New York: Doubleday, 1967.

Updike, John. *Picked-Up Pieces.* New York: Alfred A. Knopf, 1975.

Usborne, Richard. *Wodehouse at Work.* London: Herbert Jenkins, 1961.

Wall Geoffrey. *Flaubert: A Life.* New York: Farrar, Straus & Giroux, 2001.

West, James L. W. III. *William Styron: A Life.* New York: Random House, 1998.

———, ed. *Conversations with William Styron.* Jackson: University Press of Mississippi, 1985.

Wilson, A. N. *Tolstoy.* New York: W. W. Norton, 1988.

Wolf, Leonard. *The Essential Dracula.* New York: Plume, 1993.

———, ed. *The Annotated Frankenstein.* New York: Clarkson N. Potter, 1977.